EDGAR CAYCE'S ESP

EDGAR

CAYCE'S

ESP

Who He Was, What He Said, and
How It Came True

KEVIN J. TODESCHI

JEREMY P. TARCHER/PENGUIN
a member of Penguin Group (USA) Inc.
New York

JEREMY P. TARCHER/PENGUIN
Published by the Penguin Group
Penguin Group (USA) Inc., 375 Hudson Street, New York, New York 10014, USA • Penguin Group (Canada), 90 Eglinton Avenue East, Suite 700, Toronto, Ontario M4P 2Y3, Canada (a division of Pearson Canada Inc.) • Penguin Books Ltd, 80 Strand, London WC2R 0RL, England • Penguin Ireland, 25 St Stephen's Green, Dublin 2, Ireland (a division of Penguin Books Ltd) • Penguin Group (Australia), 250 Camberwell Road, Camberwell, Victoria 3124, Australia (a division of Pearson Australia Group Pty Ltd) • Penguin Books India Pvt Ltd, 11 Community Centre, Panchsheel Park, New Delhi–110 017, India • Penguin Group (NZ), 67 Apollo Drive, Rosedale, North Shore 0632, Auckland, New Zealand (a division of Pearson New Zealand Ltd) • Penguin Books (South Africa) (Pty) Ltd, 24 Sturdee Avenue, Rosebank, Johannesburg 2196, South Africa

Penguin Books Ltd, Registered Offices: 80 Strand, London WC2R 0RL, England

Most Tarcher/Penguin books are available at special quantity discounts for bulk purchase for sales promotions, premiums, fund-raising, and educational needs. Special books or book excerpts also can be created to fit specific needs. For details, write Penguin Group (USA) Inc. Special Markets, 375 Hudson Street, New York, NY 10014.

ISBN 978-1-58542-665-2

Printed in the United States of America
1 3 5 7 9 10 8 6 4 2

BOOK DESIGN BY NICOLE LAROCHE

While the author has made every effort to provide accurate telephone numbers and Internet addresses at the time of publication, neither the publisher nor the author assumes any responsibility for errors, or for changes that occur after publication. Further, the publisher does not have any control over and does not assume any responsibility for author or third-party websites or their content.

Neither the publisher nor the author is engaged in rendering professional advice or services to the individual reader. The ideas, procedures, and suggestions contained in this book are not intended as a substitute for consulting with your physician. All matters regarding your health require medical supervision. Neither the author nor the publisher shall be liable or responsible for any loss or damage allegedly arising from any information or suggestion in this book.

To Northglenn Study Group #1:

A small group of strangers who came together to study and explore the information in the Edgar Cayce readings and in the process became lifelong friends. Thank you for continuing to touch my life even now.

CONTENTS

Every single day, tens of thousands of unique users from all over the world surf the Internet to explore the life's work of one ordinary man. At any given moment, tens of thousands of people around the globe are reading in their native tongue one of hundreds of books about this man's amazing life and work. Every day, somewhere on the planet, a documentary is being broadcast highlighting some aspect of this man's incredible work. In spite of all the notoriety and attention he receives, he was an average individual in most respects: a loving husband, a father of two children, a skilled photographer, a devoted Sunday school teacher, and an eager gardener. Yet, throughout his life, he also displayed one of the most remarkable psychic talents of all time. His name was Edgar Cayce.

Daily, for more than forty years of his adult life, Cayce lay down on a couch with his hands folded over his stomach and allowed himself to enter a self-induced sleep state. Then, provided with the name and location of a person anywhere in the world, he spoke in a normal voice and gave answers to any questions about that person that he was asked. These answers, which came to be called "readings," were written down by a stenographer, who kept one copy on file and sent another to the person who had requested the information.

On file today at Edgar Cayce's Association for Research and Enlightenment, Inc., in Virginia Beach, Virginia, are copies of more than fourteen thousand psychic readings. These are available to the public and also include follow-up reports received from the people who had asked for the readings. This material represents the most massive collection of psychic information ever obtained from a single source. The organization founded by Cayce in 1931 to document, research, and disseminate his information has grown from a few hundred supporters at the time of Cayce's death in 1945 to one which is international in scope with Edgar Cayce Centers around the world. Countless people have been touched by the life's work of this man, who was raised a simple farm boy and yet became one of the most versatile and credible seers the world has ever known.

Since 1901 the information in the Cayce readings has been explored by people from every imaginable background and discipline. In addition to individuals from all walks and stations of life, the vast scope of this material has come to the attention of educators, historians, theologians, counselors, health care professionals, and scientists. No doubt, part of the attraction has been that, regardless of the field of study, Cayce has continually proven himself to have been years ahead of his time. At the dawn of the twentieth century, he was emphasizing the importance of diet, attitudes, emotions, exercise, and the patient's role—physically, mentally, and spiritually—in the treatment of illness. Inspired by the Cayce information, a group of physicians founded the American Holistic Medical Association in 1978. As a result, Cayce has been called the father of holistic medicine and has been recognized for describing the workings of the human body and foreseeing the direction of health care and much of the current treatment of illness.

In the field of psychology, he has often been compared to Carl Jung. In the realm of education, he stands with Rudolf Steiner. The Cayce information on "vibrations" as the basis of all energy and matter parallels the Superstring theory of physics. Richard H. Drummond, one of the world's most renowned theological scholars, called the Cayce information on spirituality "the finest devotional material of the twentieth century."

In history, the Cayce readings gave insights into Judaism that were verified a decade after his death with the discovery of the Dead Sea Scrolls. In world affairs, he saw the collapse of Communism nearly fifty years before it happened, and the fact that the West would eventually lose its prominence on the world economic stage to China. Repeatedly, science and history have validated concepts and ideas explored in Cayce's psychic information. The wealth of these insights has resulted in hundreds of books that explore various aspects of this man's life and work.

Just as fascinating as the breadth of the material and its

accuracy is the activity level of Cayce's mind while he was in the reading state. It was not unusual for Edgar Cayce to be giving a reading, lying on his couch, somehow mentally in touch with another person and his or her surroundings, activities, and relationships, providing answers to any question imaginable, and at the same time having a personal dream that he could recall upon awakening. Occasionally, as all this was going on, if someone in the room with Cayce thought of a question, he would respond to that person's query without even being asked! Even a casual perusal of the Cayce information makes it quite evident that the capacity of this man's mind was not limited to what we might call the conventional parameters of time and space.

Perhaps we can gain insights into this amazing talent from one of Edgar Cayce's own dreams. In 1932, while giving a reading, Cayce had a dream in which he saw himself as a tiny dot that began to be elevated as if in a whirlwind. As the dot rose, the rings of the whirlwind became larger and larger, each one encompassing a greater span of space than the one that had gone before it. There were also spaces between each ring, which the sleeping Cayce recognized as the various levels of consciousness development. A reading was given (294-131)* confirming that this experience had provided a visual

_____

* The Edgar Cayce readings are numbered to maintain confidentiality. The first set of numbers (e.g., "294") refers to the individual or group for whom the reading was given. The second set of numbers (e.g., "131") refers to the number of the reading for that individual or group.

representation of the very thing that transpired as Cayce entered the trance state. The information went on to say, "As indicated, the entity is—in the affairs of the world—a tiny speck, as it were, a mere grain of sand; yet when raised in the atmosphere or realm of the spiritual forces it becomes all inclusive…" In other words, as Cayce entered the readings state, he was no longer limited to the confines of space or time and was able to make available to himself higher levels of consciousness. It was a talent that would enable him to access insights into almost anything imaginable.

Edgar Cayce explained that once this ability was under way, his information was derived from essentially two sources: (1) the subconscious mind of the individual for whom he was giving the reading, and (2) an etheric source of information, called the "akashic records," which is apparently some kind of universal database for every thought, word, or deed that has ever transpired on Earth. The readings further described these sources:

(Q) From what source does this body Edgar Cayce derive its information?
(A) The information as given or obtained from this body is gathered from the sources from which the suggestion may derive its information.

In this state the conscious mind becomes subjugated to the subconscious, superconscious or soul mind; and may and does communicate with like minds, and the subconscious or soul force becomes universal. From any subconscious mind information may be obtained, either from this plane or from the impressions as left by the individuals that have gone on before, as we see a mirror reflecting direct that which is before it...

Through the forces of the soul, through the mind of others as presented, or that have gone on before; through the subjugation of the physical forces in this manner, the body obtains the information. 3744-3

In giving an interpretation of the records as we find them, it is well—especially for this entity—that there be given a premise from which the reasoning is drawn.

Upon time and space is written the thoughts, the deeds, the activities of an entity—as in relationships to its environs, its hereditary influence; as directed—or judgment drawn by or according to what the entity's ideal is.

Hence, as it has been oft called, the record is God's book of remembrance; and each entity, each soul—as the activities of a single day of an entity in the material world—either makes same good or bad or indifferent, depending upon the entity's application of self toward that which is the ideal manner for the use of time, opportunity, and the expression of that for which each soul enters a material manifestation.

The interpretation then as drawn here is with the desire and hope that, in opening this for the entity, the experience may be one of helpfulness and hopefulness. 1650-1

The ability to gather information in this manner may sound unusual, but even today much of the workings of the human mind remain a mystery. Some contemporary research has estimated that the brain filters out as much as 99 percent of the information available to it. Although this may seem high, how often do we become aware of the sounds made by our heating and air-conditioning systems, our own breath, or the car driving next to us in traffic? How frequently are we cognizant of the seat upon which we are sitting, the weight of our eyeglasses upon our nose, or the feeling of clothing against our skin? Do we generally let ourselves notice the intensity of colors around us or even the slight variation in smells within the rooms of our own home? Are we ever aware of the sensations upon our fingertips as we hastily type out something upon our keyboard? How many times have we driven to a familiar location and then not recalled much of the trip that actually got us there? All this information resides just beyond the bounds of conscious awareness, and yet we are not cognizant of it. Without our brain filters, we probably could not survive all the stresses, distractions, and stimuli that are simply a part of everyday life. Perhaps one component of Cayce's psychic talent was an ability to set aside the very filters that prevent our own sensory systems from being overloaded. ESP is simply an extended sense perception. With this in mind, perhaps as amazing as Cayce's extraordinary psychic ability is the fact that he was somehow able to survive and live some semblance of normalcy even while being exposed to such a vast array of incoming data.

Although the vast majority of the Cayce material deals with health and every manner of illness, countless topics were explored by Cayce's psychic talent: dreams, philosophy, intuition, business advice, the Bible, education, child rearing, ancient civilizations, personal spirituality, improving human relationships, and much more. In fact, during Cayce's lifetime he discussed an amazing ten thousand different subjects.

The Cayce legacy presents a body of information so valuable that Edgar Cayce himself might have hesitated to predict its impact on contemporary society. Who could have known that eventually terms such as *meditation, auras, spiritual growth, reincarnation,* and *holism* would become household words to millions? Edgar Cayce's A.R.E. (the Association for Research and Enlightenment, Inc.) has grown from its humble beginnings to an association with Edgar Cayce Centers in thirty-seven countries around the world. Today, the Cayce organizations consist of hundreds of educational activities and outreach programs, children's camps, a multimillion-dollar publishing company, membership benefits and services, volunteer contacts and programs worldwide, massage and health services, prison and prayer outreach programs, conferences and workshops, and affiliated schools (Atlantic University and the Cayce/Reilly School of Massotherapy).

This book has been compiled in an attempt to provide the reader with insights into Edgar Cayce's life and an overview of the types of confirmable ESP evidenced in the Edgar Cayce readings. Although not intended as an encyclopedia of every "psychic happening" in the Cayce files, it does present an amazing variety of case histories and documented stories. Even those previously unsure of the validity of psychic information will have to admit that the story of this man's life and work demands further inquiry. Perhaps it was for this very reason that Edgar Cayce himself never challenged the skeptics, preferring instead to simply extend them an invitation to "come and see."

KEVIN J. TODESCHI
Executive Director and CEO
Edgar Cayce's A.R.E.

EDGAR CAYCE'S ESP

CHAPTER I

THE STORY
OF EDGAR CAYCE

Edgar Cayce was born near Hopkinsville, Kentucky, on March 18, 1877, and had a normal childhood in many respects, one rich with the heritage of nineteenth-century farm life. The only boy in a family of five children, he grew up surrounded by grandparents, uncles, aunts, and cousins living nearby. Like many children, he had imaginary playmates, but they vanished as he grew older. He was raised at a time when much of the country was experiencing the excitement of religious revival meetings. This atmosphere may have accounted, in part, for his lifelong interest in the Bible, and even as a child, his dream was to become a medical missionary. At that early age, no one might ever have guessed the unusual manner in which his dream would become a reality.

At the age of six or seven, he told his parents that he sometimes had visions and occasionally talked to relatives who had recently died. For the most part, his family attributed these experiences to an overactive imagination and paid little attention to them. He found comfort in reading the Bible and decided to read it through from cover to cover, once for every year of his life. Its stories and characters became familiar and very real to him. At the age of thirteen, he had a vision that would influence him for the rest of his life: A beautiful woman appeared to him and asked him what he most wanted in life. He told her that, more than anything, he wanted to help others—especially children when they were sick.

Shortly after the experience, Edgar displayed a talent that could no longer be explained by his family as the boy's imagination: He could sleep on his schoolbooks and acquire a photographic memory of their entire contents! It was found that he could sleep on any book, paper, or document and, upon awakening, be able to repeat back, word for word, any length of material—even if it contained words far beyond his limited education. To be sure, the gift helped him in school, but it gradually faded. In order to help out his family financially, Edgar left school as a teenager and started working with an uncle on his grandmother's farm.

The following year, when his family moved to the city in Hopkinsville, Edgar got a job at the bookstore on Main Street. A few months later, he met and fell in love with Gertrude Evans. They became engaged on March 14, 1897, four days before Edgar's twentieth birthday, and decided to marry when he was able to support a family.

In June of 1898 Edgar lost his job and worked for a while

in a dry goods firm before moving to Louisville, Kentucky, in order to obtain a better-paying job. His goal was to raise enough money so that he and Gertrude could begin their life together. During the Christmas season of 1899 he went back to Hopkinsville and formed a partnership with his father, Leslie Cayce, who was then an insurance agent. As a result, Edgar became a traveling salesman. It was the turn of the century. He was almost twenty-three years old and seemed to be doing quite well. In addition to insurance, he sold books and stationery, and he became quite confident that it would not be long before he could afford to get married.

Unfortunately, one day, after taking a sedative in order to alleviate a headache, Edgar developed a severe case of laryngitis. At first he was not really concerned. After all, many people lose their voice for a day or two, but the condition persisted. Doctors, and later specialists, were called in, but still Edgar was unable to speak above a whisper. As the days turned into weeks, he was forced to give up his job as a salesman, and he began looking for something else he could do that did not require much speaking. Eventually, he found a job in Bowling Green as a photographer's assistant. The laryngitis persisted, and for a time Edgar gave up the idea of ever speaking normally again.

In Bowling Green, he was near Gertrude and his family, and with those closest to him nearby, it would not bother him so much that his condition was incurable. Sometimes he regretted the fact that he had never been able to finish school and become the doctor and preacher he had dreamed of becoming, but he found comfort in his loved ones and in the Bible, and he was content with the idea of settling down with a wife and children.

During the first decade of the 1900s, hypnotism and stage shows were experiencing a renewed revival in this country. One showman, who called himself Hart, the Laugh King, brought his comedy and hypnotism act to the Hopkinsville Opera House. Although not a professional therapist, Hart had witnessed some interesting experiences with hypnosis. Somehow he heard about Edgar's laryngitis and offered to try an experiment in an attempt to help the young man. In the first session, Hart hypnotized Cayce and told him that he would be able to regain his voice. To the amazement of everyone present, Edgar responded to any question asked of him in a normal voice. However, he would not take the posthypnotic suggestion, and the laryngitis returned when Hart awakened him. The experiment was repeated several times; each time, Edgar was able to speak normally in his sleep state. Nevertheless, when the young man was awakened, his soft-spoken whisper returned. Even when Hart had to leave Hopkinsville because of other commitments, Edgar's predicament was not forgotten. The local papers became excited about the case. Many people became convinced that, somehow, hypnotism was the cure for Cayce's problem.

Knowing that some patients under hypnosis showed powers of clairvoyance, a New York specialist interested in the case advised the Cayces to repeat the experiment but this time, instead of suggesting that the young man's voice return, to ask Edgar himself to talk about his condition. His parents were against the idea. Ever since the first experiment with Hart, their son had lost weight. It appeared as though the sessions were a drain on his physical body. Gertrude let her fiancé make the decision, for with or without his voice, they could have a life together—and besides, Edgar rather liked working with photography. In the end, Edgar consented to one further test.

A local man, Al Layne, was found to give the hypnotic suggestions. Layne had educated himself. Not only had he worked with hypnotism, but he was familiar with osteopathy as well. Edgar offered to put himself to sleep—much as he had done when he had slept on his schoolbooks. Once Edgar was asleep on the couch, Layne asked him to explain what was wrong with him and how he could be cured. And Cayce spoke back!

While asleep, Edgar Cayce described his problem as a "psychological condition producing a physical effect." He went on to explain that the condition could be removed by suggesting to him while he was in the unconscious state that the blood circulation increase to the affected areas. After Layne made the suggestion, he and Cayce's family watched in amazement as the upper part of Edgar's chest and his throat turned a bright crimson and the skin became warm to the touch. Twenty minutes passed before Edgar spoke again, stating that before Layne awakened him, the suggestion should be made that the blood circulation return to normal. Layne followed the instructions. When Cayce finally awakened, he was able to speak normally for the first time in almost a year. The date, March 31, 1901, would become known as the first time Edgar Cayce officially gave a psychic reading.

Edgar, his parents, and Gertrude were overjoyed that he could finally talk. The young man's plan was to continue being a photographer, and to get married as soon as possible. He would never have given another thought to putting himself into the sleep state, except that Al Layne had witnessed something truly extraordinary and was beginning to have other ideas.

For years Layne had been bothered by a stomach difficulty that doctors had been unable to cure. Because he knew enough about medicine to realize which therapeutic suggestions could be harmful, he asked Edgar to try giving a reading on the stomach problem. Although skeptical, Edgar agreed. He felt obligated to Layne for having helped him regain his voice. The reading was given to satisfy Layne's curiosity. Asleep on the couch, Cayce spoke in a normal voice and described the problem exactly; he recommended herbal medicines, foods, and exercises for improvement. After one week of following the sleeping Cayce's suggestions, Layne felt so much better that he became even more excited about Edgar's ability, and he strongly encouraged the young man to try other tests.

With this turn of events, Edgar Cayce felt as if he had been placed in a precarious position. On the one hand, this business of readings was very strange to him. He knew nothing about medicine or the diagnosing of illness or even the workings of psychic ability. He only wanted to live a normal life in Hopkinsville with a wife and a family. On the other hand, Layne argued that Cayce had a moral obligation if his talent could be helpful to people. Finally, after a great deal of prayer, after talking it over with his family, and after looking to his Bible for guidance, Edgar agreed to continue the experiments under two conditions: The first was that, if he ever suggested anything in the sleep state that could be at all harmful to people, he would stop the readings; the second was that Layne had to always remember that Edgar Cayce was, first and foremost, a photographer.

One of the earliest readings was for a six-year-old girl, named Aimee Dietrich, who had been seriously ill for three years. At the age of two, after an attack of influenza, which doctors then called the grippe, her mind had stopped developing. Since that time, her tiny body had been racked with convulsions. Her mind was nearly a blank, and though doctors and specialists had been consulted, she had only gotten worse instead of better.

In order to see if he could be of assistance, Cayce put himself to sleep while Layne conducted the reading and wrote down everything that was said. While in the sleep state, Cayce stated that Aimee's real problem had actually begun a few days before catching the grippe. Apparently, she had fallen and injured her spine while getting down from a carriage. According to the reading, because of the trauma, the influenza germs had settled in her spine, and the convulsions had begun. Aimee's mother verified the accident.

To cure the condition, Edgar Cayce recommended some osteopathic adjustments that were to be carried out by Layne. Layne made the adjustments on the little girl's spine and got a "check" reading. The sleeping Cayce told Layne that he had made the adjustments incorrectly and provided further instructions. After several attempts, Layne was able to carry out the suggestions to the exact specifications of the sleeping photographer. Several days later Aimee recognized a doll she had played with before getting sick and called it by name. As the weeks passed, her mind recognized other things as well, she suddenly knew her parents, and the convulsions stopped completely. Within three months Aimee's mind caught up with her physical age, and she became a normal, healthy, six-year-old girl.

Cayce was truly happy that he had been able to help, but still he wanted only to live a normal life. However, Layne's enthusiasm, along with the enthusiasm of Cayce's own father and people like Mr. and Mrs. Dietrich, made it all the more difficult to leave the "psychic business" behind. Cayce continued giving readings without charge, while Layne conducted. It was soon discovered that Cayce needed only the name and location of an individual to be able to give a reading, diagnose the person's condition, and outline a regimen of treatment. The readings puzzled him. Many times he did not even understand what he had said after he had awakened and Layne showed him what had been written down. Edgar agreed to continue, however, if somehow his unusual gift could be helpful to people.

In addition to his job and his work with the readings, Edgar decided the time had come to get married. On June 17, 1903, after an engagement of more than six years, Gertrude Evans and Edgar Cayce finally became husband and wife. They made a home together in Bowling Green, Kentucky. Although still somewhat uncomfortable with the readings, Edgar found life fulfilling. He had a loving wife, a home, a Sunday school class at the local church, and a good job. A year later he formed his own photography partnership and was able to open a studio.

Eventually, Layne decided to become a fully accredited osteopath. The number of patients coming to him had continued to increase as he and Cayce had become well known. To continue his studies, Layne left Hopkinsville and entered the Southern School of Osteopathy. But Cayce's belief that Layne's departure meant that the readings might be put to rest for a time was short-lived.

Edgar spent most of his time working as a photographer. The studio was prosperous. Unfortunately, disaster occurred when a studio fire destroyed a large collection of prints and reproductions that Cayce had borrowed on consignment.

Suddenly he was deeply in debt. Nine months later a second fire destroyed the studio. Edgar stayed in Bowling Green to pay off his debts. Gertrude returned to Hopkinsville with Hugh Lynn, their son, who was born on March 16, 1907. Eventually, Edgar looked for work in Alabama, where photographers were scarce.

During one of Edgar's return visits to Hopkinsville, Leslie Cayce introduced his son to Dr. Wesley Ketchum, M.D., a homeopath who had just moved to town. Dr. Ketchum had heard of Cayce through some of Layne's former patients and had decided to get a reading for himself. Unbeknownst to Cayce, Ketchum had recently diagnosed himself as having early problems with appendicitis. The doctor wanted to see if Cayce could pick up on the problem. However, while asleep, Cayce gave an entirely different diagnosis and outlined a simple treatment. In order to humor the young man, Dr. Ketchum went to another doctor for a third opinion and was surprised to discover that Cayce's diagnosis and not his own had been correct!

As a result, Dr. Ketchum started using Cayce's psychic talent in some of his most difficult medical cases. In one of the early cases, a construction supervisor named Dalton severely fractured his leg and kneecap in an accident. He was told by several doctors in town that they could set the leg, but because of the seriousness of the injury, he would never be able to walk normally again. Apparently, Dalton's kneecap was damaged beyond repair. Not satisfied with their reports,

Dalton consulted Dr. Wesley Ketchum. Cayce gave a reading and recommended what was an extremely radical treatment for the time: Ketchum was to drive several roofing nails into the kneecap to hold it in place while it healed. The procedure was unheard of, but Ketchum, trusting in Cayce's ability, carried it out. The surgery was performed, and several months later Dalton was up and walking around as though the accident had never occurred. Edgar Cayce's fame continued to spread.

In 1910 Wesley Ketchum submitted a paper to the American Society of Clinical Research, calling Cayce a medical wonder. As a result, the October 9 issue of the *New York Times* featured a long article on Cayce's ability. The headline read: ILLITERATE MAN BECOMES A DOCTOR WHEN HYPNOTIZED. Requests for readings began coming to Hopkinsville. In order to meet those requests, Dr. Wesley Ketchum, Edgar Cayce, Leslie Cayce, and Albert Noe, a hotel owner, formed the Psychic Reading Corporation. Edgar moved back to Hopkinsville, where he opened a photography studio, the Cayce Art Studio. He began to give readings in his spare time and became known as a "psychic diagnostician," although he was much happier as a photographer. It would not be until the following year that his attitude about the readings finally changed.

A second son was born to Gertrude and Edgar in 1911. They named him Milton Porter. Soon after his birth, however, the baby developed whooping cough and, later, colitis.

Several doctors were called in, but the baby continued to get worse. For some reason Edgar Cayce never really thought about consulting his own readings until the doctors had given up all hope. As a last resort, Cayce gave a reading for his second son. When he woke up, he was shattered to learn that the condition was too serious. The readings offered no hope for the child, and the baby died before he was two months old.

Afterward, Cayce and his wife went into a state of depression. He blamed himself for not getting a reading sooner. Perhaps it might have helped; now he would never know. Gertrude's health took a turn for the worse. She became weak after the baby's death, causing the doctor to think she had contracted pleurisy. As the months passed, the illness hung on, and she showed no signs of improvement. In fact, she was getting worse and was eventually confined to bed.

By late summer Gertrude's doctor had changed his diagnosis. He called Cayce aside and spoke the awful truth: Gertrude had tuberculosis and was dying. A specialist confirmed that nothing further could be done. Everyone expected her to die by the end of the year, except for her husband. Not knowing what else to do, Edgar gave a reading. While in the sleep state, he recommended a combination of prescription drugs as well as filling a charred oak keg with apple brandy. Gertrude was to inhale the fumes to clear up the congestion. Although the doctors claimed that the combination of drugs would be useless, Dr. Ketchum wrote the prescription anyway. After following this treatment for only two days, Gertrude felt better, and her fever had fallen. By September she was better still, and by November even her doctors decided that she was going to get well. By the first of January 1912 Gertrude Cayce was fully recovered.

That same year, a delegate from Harvard University, Dr. Hugo Münsterberg, investigated Edgar Cayce. The purpose of the visit had been to determine whether or not Cayce's work was fraudulent, but by the time Münsterberg left Hopkinsville, he had become convinced of the legitimacy and effectiveness of the readings. Still, Edgar was happiest being a photographer, and he decided to dissolve his partnership with Ketchum, his father, and Noe. He obtained a job as a photographer in Selma, Alabama. The following year he bought for himself the studio where he had been employed.

In Selma, Cayce was able to escape from the readings' notoriety and live a quiet life, but that normalcy did not last long. One day his son, Hugh Lynn, was playing with flash powder in the studio and severely burned his eyes. The local doctors gave no hope that the boy would ever see again. In fact, they said he was blinded in one eye, and they recommended removing the other eye due to the extent of the damage. Cayce decided to give a reading instead. During the course of the reading, he gave assurance that sight was not gone. He recommended an additional compound to be added to the solution that had been prescribed by the doctors and stated that Hugh Lynn should remain in a darkened room for two weeks with his eyes bandaged. No eye surgery was performed, and when the bandages were removed, the boy could see. Local newspapers picked up the story, and again Edgar Cayce's fame grew. In addition to his job and his work as a Sunday school teacher, he once again began giving readings. On February 9, 1918, Gertrude gave birth to another son, Edgar Evans.

As Cayce's reputation as a psychic grew, the request for readings continued and he was faced with a problem. Although people were being helped by the readings, many were having difficulty finding doctors to carry out the treatments that were being recommended. Doctors seemed hesitant to follow the guidance of a sleeping psychic who, in many instances, had never even seen the people he was diagnosing. This situation led to Cayce's dream of establishing a hospital, staffed with fully qualified doctors, nurses, and therapists, who would carry out the treatments recommended in the readings.

This pursuit of a hospital caused Edgar Cayce to form an ill-fated partnership with others who were seeking oil. He went to Texas to give readings on possible oil sites but was repeatedly disappointed. The readings made it quite clear that the information was never to be used for financial gain and that some of his partners did not share his dream of a hospital. Some wanted the money only for themselves. After repeated failures to find oil, Cayce returned to Selma and picked up where he had left off. He had his wife, his two sons, his business, and the church. His Sunday school classes became the most popular in the county because Cayce had the ability to make the Bible come alive. In the fall of 1923 he hired a secretary, Gladys Davis, to take down the information in the readings, while Gertrude conducted them and asked her sleeping husband the questions.

Until 1923 most of Cayce's readings were limited to medical and physical conditions. That year, however, a printer from Dayton, Ohio, who had obtained successful readings for two of his nieces, asked Cayce for a horoscope reading. Toward the end of the reading (5717-1) the sleeping Cayce spoke the curious sentence: "He was once a monk." That statement opened the door to a whole new area of research— the possibility of reincarnation—and Edgar was faced with a new dilemma.

There was no doubt that the information was helpful and accurate when dealing with health, but the readings' matter-of-fact reference to reincarnation seemed foreign to his fundamentalist view of Christianity. He prayed about it, did much soul searching, and obtained a few readings. He was advised to read the Bible once more from cover to cover while keeping the idea of reincarnation in mind. The underlying philosophy that emerged was one that focused upon the oneness and the purposefulness of life. In time Cayce found that the concept of reincarnation was not incompatible with any religion and actually merged perfectly with his own beliefs of what it meant to be a Christian.

Soon afterward, he began giving what he called "life

readings," dealing with an individual's previous lifetimes, as well as the person's potential and purpose in the present. In time the topics in the readings were further expanded to include mental and spiritual counsel, philosophy and contemporary spirituality, meditation, dream interpretation, intuition, history and ancient civilizations, and even advice for improving personal relationships.

Because the requests for readings continued to grow, Cayce gave up his photography studio and began looking for financial backing for his hospital. He also began to accept payment directly for the readings, but he never refused to help those who were unable to pay. Over the years, several backers were found to make Cayce's dream of the hospital a reality. One group wanted to locate the facility in Chicago; another wanted it to be in Dayton, to where the Cayces had moved. However, time and again the readings advised that the hospital needed to be located in or near Virginia Beach, Virginia. Finally, a New York businessman, Morton Blumenthal, agreed to finance the hospital project where the readings advised.

In September 1925 the Cayce family moved, with Gladys Davis, to Virginia Beach, and in 1927 the Association of National Investigators was formed. Its purpose was to research and experiment with the information contained in the readings. Its motto was "That We May Make Manifest the Love of God and Man." The following year, on November 11, 1928, the Edgar Cayce Hospital opened its doors.

Patients came from all over the country to obtain readings and to be treated by a qualified staff composed of doctors, nurses, and therapists. The sleeping Cayce gave each patient a reading, diagnosed the ailment, and recommended everything from a change of diet to surgery. Cayce's approach was that healing worked best when all the schools of medicine worked together in cooperation, finding what was best for the patient.

In spite of the stock market crash in October 1929, Atlantic University, also underwritten by the hospital backers, opened in the fall of 1930 as Virginia Beach, Virginia's first university. Until 1931 the hospital operated successfully. In the midst of the Depression, however, financial backing was lost, and the hospital had to close its doors in February. The university survived until Christmas.

In July 1931 a new group, the Association for Research and Enlightenment, Inc. (A.R.E.), was formed as a research body whose goal was to investigate and disseminate the information contained in Cayce's readings. This organization became interested in such things as holistic health care, the workings of ESP, meditation, spiritual healing, the importance of dreams, and the study of life after death. When individuals asked Edgar Cayce how they could become more psychic themselves, he responded by saying that the goal should be to become more spiritual, "For the psychic is of the soul." From Cayce's perspective, as individuals became more spiritual, psychic ability would develop naturally. Rather than trying to find converts to the readings' philosophy, people were told that if they could incorporate the information into their own religious and belief systems, enabling them to become better people, it could be a useful and positive experience; otherwise, they were advised to leave the information alone.

As the years passed, Cayce became more and more psychic in the waking state as well. He once fled from a room in sorrow because he knew that three young men would not be returning from the war. He also had developed the ability to see auras—fields of light that surround all living things. From these auras, Cayce could perceive people's moods as well as their overall physical condition.

As his fame as a psychic grew, so did the number of skeptics. Many people came to Virginia Beach to expose him as a fraud, but in time all were convinced of the legitimacy of what he was doing. A number stayed in Virginia Beach and received readings for themselves. One staunchly Catholic writer, Thomas Sugrue, came to Virginia Beach to investigate what he thought had to be trickery and ended up writing *There Is a River*, the highly successful Cayce biography, published in 1943 while Cayce was still alive. *Coronet* magazine, one of the most popular of the era, sent a reporter to investigate. The article, "Miracle Man of Virginia Beach," written by Marguerite Harmon Bro, drew widespread attention, and Edgar Cayce became more famous than he had ever been before.

During the height of World War II, sacks of mail were

delivered to Cayce with ever-growing requests for readings. Despite the readings' warning that he should give no more than two readings each day, Cayce began giving up to eight in an effort to keep up with requests. Gladys Davis's appointment book had readings scheduled two years in advance!

In the spring of 1944 Edgar began to grow weaker. His own readings advised him to rest, but he felt a tremendous obligation to those who were asking for his help. Finally he collapsed from sheer exhaustion, and just as his first reading had been for himself, his last reading was for himself, given in September 1944. The reading again told him he had to rest. When Gertrude asked, "How long?" the response was "Until [he] is well or dead." Shortly afterward, he had a stroke and became partially paralyzed. By the end of the year, his friends feared the worst. Although Edgar told them he would be healed after the first of the year, they understood what he meant, and he died on January 3, 1945. At the time, no one really realized how ill Gertrude also was, and within three months, on Easter Sunday, she died as well.

Gladys Davis took it upon herself to preserve the information, which she had taken such great pains to write down, until Edgar's sons returned from the war. Eventually, she took charge of the project of cataloguing and indexing the more than fourteen thousand readings. Because of the number of readings, as well as the follow-up reports and other documentation, the project was not finished until 1971, more than a quarter of a century after Cayce died! Once they were indexed, it was discovered that the readings covered an aston-ishing ten thousand different subjects—nearly every ques-tion imaginable had been asked. Gladys continued working as secretary for the A.R.E. Board of Trustees and chaired the group that tackled the computerization of the readings until her death in 1986 at the age of eighty-one. Today, in addition to their headquarters in Virginia Beach, Virginia, the com-plete set of Edgar Cayce readings is available electronically, online, and at Edgar Cayce centers worldwide.

With his return from the war, Hugh Lynn Cayce took over the organization his father had started and was able to encourage interest all over the world. When Hugh Lynn died in 1982, the Association had grown from a few hun-dred members to tens of thousands with outreach activities around the globe. That growth has continued so that today several organizations work with the information contained in the Cayce readings. Edgar Cayce's A.R.E. continues to make the material more readily available through practical presentations, publications, research, activities, and online materials (EdgarCayce.org) and members throughout the world are kept up-to-date on activities and developments concerning the Cayce work. The Edgar Cayce Foundation is a separate organization that is legally responsible for the readings. Atlantic University was reactivated in 1985, and today offers a master's degree in transpersonal studies. The Cayce/Reilly School of Massotherapy trains therapists from around the world in many of the healing protocols contained in the Cayce readings, as well as the therapeutic benefits of massage. Together, these organizations have found that the psychic information of a photographer from Kentucky has stood the test of decades of intensive exploration, research, and application.

Throughout his life, Edgar Cayce claimed no special abilities; nor did he ever consider himself to be some kind of twentieth-century prophet. The readings never offered a set of beliefs that had to be embraced but instead focused on the fact that each person should test in his or her own life the principles presented. Though Cayce himself was a Christian and read the entire Bible every year of his life, his Work stressed the importance of comparative study among belief systems all over the world. The underlying principle of the readings is the oneness of all life, tolerance for all people, and a compassion and understanding for every religion in the world.

CHAPTER 2

AN OVERVIEW OF THE
EDGAR CAYCE MATERIAL

From about the age of twenty-four, Edgar Cayce demonstrated the uncanny ability to put himself into some kind of self-induced sleep state where his mind was in contact with all time and space. From this state of deep relaxation and meditation, he could respond to questions as diverse as "What is my purpose in life?" and "How can I heal my relationships?" to "How can I cure my psoriasis?" and "What is the meaning of this dream?" His responses to these questions came to be called "readings" and contained insights so valuable that, even to this day, people continue to find practical help for everything from maintaining a well-balanced diet and improving human relationships to overcoming life-threatening illnesses and experiencing a closer relationship with God.

The majority of Edgar Cayce's readings deal with health maintenance and the treatment of illness. Even to this day, people still find physical help from this wealth of information. Yet although he was best known for this material, the sleeping Cayce did not seem to be limited to concerns about the physical body. In fact, in their entirety, the readings discuss an astonishing ten thousand different subjects. Even this vast array of subject matter, however, can be narrowed down into a much smaller range of categories and topics.

The readings themselves have been divided into several categories: one called *physical readings* or *health readings*, totaling more than 9,600; life readings, numbering more than 1,900 that deal with reincarnation, an individual's soul strengths and weaknesses, and one's purpose for being on the earth at this time; and more than 2,700 *special readings*, including various series of readings given on such topics as business, dreams, soul growth, spiritual healing, the work of Cayce's Association, world affairs, ancient civilizations, and mental and spiritual advice. Some of the most popular subjects fall under five themes: (1) health and healing; (2) philosophy and reincarnation; (3) dreams and dream interpretation; (4) ESP and psychic phenomena; and (5) spiritual growth.

THE READINGS' APPROACH
TO HEALTH AND HEALING

The information from the readings on health includes simple suggestions that each of us can do to stay well. The nature of many of these recommendations indicates that Cayce's understanding of the workings of the human body was decades ahead of its time. His basic health principles include such things as maintaining a well-balanced diet, the need for regular exercise, the role of attitudes and emotions in achieving and maintaining good health, the importance of relaxation and recreation as part of a balanced lifestyle, and the desirability of keeping our physical bodies cleansed on the inside as well as on the outside.

Essentially, Cayce's approach to staying well has its roots in health maintenance and preventive medicine rather than simply treating illness as it occurs. He was one of the first in the Western Hemisphere to recommend a nutritious diet consisting mainly of vegetables, fish, and fowl, plus sufficient water each day to promote internal cleansing. These guidelines and others were recommended by Cayce at a time when much of the country had a diet consisting of great quantities of red meat and starches. Yet Cayce's contribution to health and physical well-being was not limited to proper diet and regular exercise.

Decades ago he emphasized the importance that attitudes and emotions play in physical well-being. Clinical medicine, on the other hand, has only relatively recently discovered how positive attitudes enhance the healing process. Both the Cayce information and modern medicine now agree that humor and joy play key roles in facilitating wellness. It has also been found that certain kinds of negative attitudes or stresses can lead to illness. For example, Cayce's readings suggested that persistent anger—whether conscious or unconscious—plays a part in the onset of some diseases.

Even critics of other segments of Cayce's work agree that the information on health offers important insights into how each of us can stay well. The readings made recommendations for a variety of health concerns—from acne, diabetes, hemorrhoids, longevity, and warts, to arthritis, cancer, epilepsy, mental illness, and psoriasis. Nearly every condition that existed between 1900 and 1945, whether it was childbirth, fractures, or a vitamin deficiency, is represented in the Cayce files. Interestingly enough, modern-day researchers have found that many of the recommended treatments given decades ago by the sleeping Cayce to specific individuals seem to be applicable today on a much-wider scale. The information on psoriasis and scleroderma are two of the most notable examples. For both of these diseases, the Cayce regimen involves specific dietary changes, particular spinal adjustments, and other natural remedy procedures. In recent years hundreds of people with these two ailments have been helped by following a similar regimen of treatment. Medical research has even confirmed what Cayce said decades ago: that psoriasis appears to be caused by permeability of the intestines.

The readings were given between 1901 and 1944, and many were ahead of their time in foreseeing future approaches to health care. In addition to insights into energy medicine, the role of attitudes and emotions, and the effects of prayer and spiritual healing, Cayce also saw total health as involving coordination among the physical, mental, and spiritual components of life. For any complete approach to health, it is necessary to consider an individual's entire being rather than simply the illness. Because of this concept, it has been said that the beginnings of present-day holistic health really started with Edgar Cayce.

A reading for a person asking for physical help was given much like the others. Cayce put himself to sleep on his couch, while his secretary, Gladys Davis, sat nearby with her steno pad and prepared to write down everything that was said. The person conducting the reading, usually Cayce's wife, Gertrude, gave him the proper suggestion for obtaining the information that was needed. For physical readings, her suggestion to the sleeping Cayce went something like this:

> You will have before you the body of [Gertrude would then say the person's name], who is located at [the city and address]. You will go over the body carefully, examine it thoroughly, and tell me the conditions you find at the present time; giving the cause of the existing conditions, also the suggestions for the help and relief for this body. You will speak distinctly at a normal rate of speech. You will answer the questions that may be asked.

Then, while he was sleeping, Cayce generally responded with "Yes, we have the body here." If he had ever given a prior reading for the person, he added, "This we have had before," even if the person's last reading had been years earlier. Cayce picked up right where he had left off, as if no time had passed. He spoke in his own voice and referred to the person as if the individual were in the same room, even though Cayce was usually in Virginia Beach and the patient could be a thousand miles or more away. He then gave a general description of the person's condition, including information about the blood supply, the nervous system, and the organs involved in the difficulty. Finally he outlined detailed methods to bring about relief and responded to questions as they were asked. If the person getting the reading was in the same room with Edgar Cayce, she or he only needed to think of the question and Cayce would answer it without even being asked.

The major components of the readings' approach to wellness can be incorporated into an acronym: CARE—circulation, assimilation, relaxation, and elimination. First proposed by Dr. Harold J. Reilly, a longtime proponent of the Cayce health information, each of these components has particular importance in the readings:

- Without proper *circulation*, the body's ability to heal itself is severely impaired. The natural healing process is bolstered by improving the blood circulation—through exercise, massage, and other manipulative therapies, such as chiropractic and osteopathic adjustments.
- *Assimilation* is the second key word. It is the body's ability to digest and distribute food, minerals, and vitamins. One

aspect of assimilation takes into account an individual's diet—which the readings suggest should consist of 20 percent acid-producing to 80 percent alkaline-producing foods, as well as eight glasses of water daily. But assimilation is also influenced by the methods in which our foods are prepared and the ways in which we combine them. For example, although both grain cereals and citrus fruits are to be included in a healthful diet, the readings suggest that they are never to be eaten during the same meal because of their negative effect, when combined, on the body's digestion. The importance of food combining was another major factor in Cayce's readings.

- The third key word is *relaxation*, which includes not only getting enough sleep but also setting time aside for recreation. Cayce told one person:

  ... these [conditions] arose as a result of what might be called occupational disturbances; not enough in the sun, not enough of hard work. Plenty of brain work, but the body is supposed to coordinate the spiritual, mental and physical. He who does not give recreation a place in his life, and the proper tone to each phase—well, he just fools self and will some day ... be paying the price. 3352-1

- The final component of CARE is *elimination*. Proper eliminations are necessary for the body to rid itself of toxins, cleanse the internal organs, and function normally. Long before folks were talking about their regularity, Cayce advised people not to let a day pass without having thrown off waste products. Ways to help facilitate this process include such practices as proper diet, exercise (such as walking), sweat baths, colonics, correct breathing, and plenty of water.

Taken together, these four components of a healthy lifestyle—circulation, assimilation, relaxation, and elimination—can help promote healing, wellness, and longevity.

It is important to note that the Cayce information on health and healing contains far more than simple approaches to health maintenance and wellness. The readings recommend surgery, prescription medications, physical manipulations, energy work, physical therapy, dietary and attitudinal changes, prayer—you name it. Cayce's approach was that each of the health-care fields had something important to contribute to healing the human body. The essential purpose of any healing technique, however, was to enable the body to return to a state of physical wholeness and an ultimate awareness of the individual's connection to the divine. In the language of the readings:

> For, all healing comes from the one source. And whether there is the application of foods, exercise, medicine, or even the knife—it is to bring the consciousness of the forces within the body that aid in reproducing themselves—the awareness of creative or God forces. 2696-1

It should be emphasized that Edgar Cayce never provided magic formulas or miracle cures. While it is true that miracles of healing can happen, the readings usually recommended an overall regimen of therapies involving the whole system. Cayce was not a psychic healer; he claimed no special power. Instead, he gave psychic counseling for total health, instructing people in what they could do to best bring about their own healing. Following the regimen often took a lot of effort. On occasion, when someone requested medical assistance for a condition, Cayce would respond with "Why do you want to get well?" In other words, if after health improvement, the patient simply returned to the same lifestyle that had led to the sickness in the first place, then the person was simply looking for ways to alleviate symptoms rather than getting to the real heart of the illness.

THE READINGS' APPROACH TO
PHILOSOPHY AND REINCARNATION

In 1901, at the age of twenty-four, Edgar Cayce gave the first reading for himself, diagnosing a health condition, but it wasn't until 1923 that the subject of reincarnation was explored in a reading given to a printer from Ohio. Interestingly enough, the concept had been mentioned in a prior reading in 1911, but no one among Cayce's associates was familiar with the idea, and the reference wasn't recognized as such for decades. Eventually, the subject was examined in extensive detail in nineteen hundred life readings, becoming the second major topic examined by the sleeping Cayce.

Just what is reincarnation? It is the process in which each of us goes through a series of lifetimes for the purpose of spiritual growth and soul development. Cayce's approach does not include the concept of transmigration, a related theory that it is possible for human beings to be born again as animals. From the standpoint of the Cayce material, souls occupy only human bodies through their spiritual growth and development.

In essence, the Cayce approach to reincarnation provides a philosophical setting to the past but focuses on practical ways of dealing with this life: living, growing, and being of service to one another in the present. For him, it wasn't nearly so important who people had once been or even what they had done as it was paramount that they focus on the present and the opportunities and challenges that face them in this time, in this place, right now.

From the Cayce readings' perspective, the past merely provided a framework of potentials and probabilities. An individual's choices, actions, and free will in the present determine the actual experience lived this time around. Rather than being a fatalistic approach to life, this approach recognizes a lifetime as much more one of nearly limitless opportunities.

Edgar Cayce, however, was also familiar with the less positive aspects of the philosophy of reincarnation. He contended that some approaches create a misunderstanding of the real purpose behind the soul experiencing a series of lifetimes. In fact, an approach to reincarnation that did not take into account freedom of choice created what he called a karmic "bugaboo" (1436-3)—a misunderstanding that provided no arena for the real action and interconnectedness that exist among karma, free will, destiny, and grace. In his understanding, people were very much active participants in their individual life's journey and not at all simply sometime-reluctant observers.

However, even to this day, the theory of reincarnation is often misinterpreted as a fatalistic journey through experiences and relationships that are ours because of our "karma." In this approach, choices we have made in the past have somehow etched in stone our futures, and life is simply a process of going through the motions. This is definitely not the Cayce approach to karma.

The word *karma* is a Sanskrit term that means "work, deed, or act"; it has also been interpreted to mean "cause and effect." Although the readings definitely agree with this concept, perhaps one of their most intriguing and unique philosophical contributions is the idea that karma can simply be defined as memory. It is not really a debt that must be paid according to some universal tally sheet, nor is it necessarily a set of specific circumstances that must be experienced because of deeds or misdeeds from the past. Karma is simply memory. It is a pool of information that the subconscious mind draws upon and utilizes in the present. It has elements that are positive as well as those that might seem negative. For example, an immediate affinity toward another individual is as likely to be karmic, as is an immediate animosity toward someone else. To be sure, this subconscious memory has an effect and influence on how we think, how we react, what we choose, and even what we look like! But the component of free will is ever within our grasp.

In Cayce's explanation of reincarnation, when an individual dies, the next lifetime does not occur immediately, for the soul is given a chance to take stock of all it has come to know. Then it has the opportunity to decide for itself what lessons it needs to learn next in order to become a more complete individual. The soul chooses to be born again into the earth, generally among at least some people it has known before. A soul can decide to be born as either a male or female in any given lifetime, or, as Cayce often called it, an "incarnation." The choices made are such that the soul might best fulfill the specific purpose chosen for that particular lifetime. It selects those surroundings (parents and family, location, and time period, etc.) that will best allow for the learning of those lessons it needs for completeness. The goal is to express love fully in all the challenges that physical life offers. Our life experiences, however, are always subject to the choices we make with our own free will.

With our free will, we can turn the challenges that life presents to us into stepping-stones toward growth, or we can see them as obstacles and stumbling blocks. Either way, we reap what we have sown. From Cayce's perspective, we constantly meet the consequences of previous deeds and attitudes.

One of the interesting aspects about reincarnation is that talents and skills are never lost. Someone who has developed an ability in one life will still have it to draw upon later. For example, many child prodigies with a talent, let's say for music, are born with a conscious recollection of this ability that was developed in an earlier lifetime. If a person happens to be an excellent English teacher in this life, she or he may have been a playwright in the last, a historian before that, and perhaps a scribe even earlier. One's abilities are channeled in those directions that will best help that person fulfill the purpose of a particular lifetime.

Another major philosophical contribution the Cayce readings provide is the idea that there really isn't karma between people; instead, there is only karma with one's own self. The conceptual challenge, however, is that we seem to most effectively come to terms with our own karmic memory or "meet ourselves" through our interactions with others. It is this interesting dynamic of meeting ourselves through our relationships with other individuals that oftentimes causes us to perceive them as the basis of our frustrations and challenges, rather than accepting the responsibility as our own.

Yet, in spite of the fact that our karma is essentially ours, we are constantly drawn toward certain individuals and groups that will enable us to meet ourselves in probable circumstances and relationships. They, in turn, are drawn toward us in an effort to come to terms with their own karmic memory as well. Interestingly enough, it is how each individual decides to "meet self," one choice at a time, that will essentially determine the life she or he experiences in the present.

These karmic groups often reestablish themselves in terms of family relationships, work and cultural ties, and even associations on a national level. Cayce stated that we never meet anyone by chance; nor do we ever have an emotional connection (positive or negative) with another person for the very first time. Relationships are an ongoing learning and experiential process.

Within this framework of lessons that need to be learned as the soul strives to meet itself is the central idea that the soul is constantly experiencing the consequences of its previous choices. This concept is expressed in biblical terminology as "What you sow, you must reap" and is generally labeled "Like attracts like" by students of reincarnation.

Essentially, what this means is that we get to experience for ourselves the effects our previous choices have had upon others. Rather than our lives being predestined or fatalistic in nature, we continue to be in control of them (and our perceptions) through how we choose to respond to the life situations that we've drawn to us. With this in mind, ultimately, all experiences are for our own good and growth, and all experiences are of our own creation.

In practical terms, we may not always be able to understand why a certain situation was drawn to us, and in fact the "why" may not be of primary importance. What is important is how we choose to respond. For example, two people might face very similar circumstances—let's say, the loss of a job—yet each person might deal with the situation in a very different manner. One might spend a great deal of time and energy becoming bitter and angry over what happened, and the other might see it as a wonderful opportunity to start all over and do something which has always been a desire. Although the situation is the same, each person's response is quite different. The way a person responds to a situation determines the next cycle or experience called into action.

Reincarnation is a concept large enough to encompass not only Eastern thought but all of the major religions of the world. As the great leveler of humankind, it is a concept that can allow us to have more compassion for one another. It provides a way in which we can begin to look at all facets of life as having a purpose. However, it doesn't really matter if another person believes or doubts the theory of rebirth. For some, it can be a helpful concept; for others, it might be confusing. The reason for believing in reincarnation is not so that we can dwell upon the past or brag about the possibility of once having been someone famous. The wisest student of reincarnation knows that we have all had incarnations in both lowly and lofty circumstances. Instead, Cayce summed up the purpose this way:

In the studies, then, know *where* ye are going.

... to find that ye only lived, died and were buried under the cherry tree in Grandmother's garden does not make thee one whit better neighbor, citizen, mother or father!

But to know that ye spoke unkindly and suffered for it and in the present may correct it by being righteous—*that* is worthwhile! 5753-2

THE READINGS' APPROACH TO DREAMS
AND DREAM INTERPRETATION

Although it is true that many of us do not make a conscious effort to remember our dreams, everyone does dream. During the early part of this century, while psychologists such as Sigmund Freud and Carl Jung were demonstrating the clinical importance of dreams, Edgar Cayce was providing average people with guidelines for one of the most practical approaches to working with dreams. Hundreds of Cayce's readings deal with the subject of dreams and dream interpretation. Perhaps the most important insight gained from the wealth of this material is the fact that each of us at subconscious levels is aware of much more than we realize when we're awake about ourselves, our physical bodies, our surroundings, our relationships, even our future.

In the dream state, we open our minds to many different levels of our own unconscious. Not only are all of our previous conscious experiences retained there, but it is also the storehouse of resources that rarely come to conscious awareness. The unconscious has remarkable talents for finding solutions to problems. It houses all of our wishes, hopes, and memories of past experiences, and can also assist us with self-examination, providing practical guidance for any question. It even makes it possible for us to have psychic experiences.

Dreams can diagnose the causes of our physical ailments, point out the thoughts and emotions that we've tried to overlook, and often make suggestions for improving our relationships with others. While dreaming, we can gain awareness about our entire being: physically, mentally, and spiritually.

It was Carl Jung, a Swiss psychiatrist and contemporary of Edgar Cayce's, who found convincing evidence for a deep level to the unconscious mind. This profound depth, Jung felt, came from genuine spiritual reality that hadn't been acknowledged by Freud. Jung called this level the collective unconscious. Here, all minds could communicate through the use of universal symbols—images which seem to have a common meaning among people all over the world. For example, a symbol such as a lion or a great cat has a universal or archetypal meaning of power and vitality. Water is often suggestive of spirit or emotion. An old man, an old woman, or a grandparental figure can symbolize our own "higher self" or our own internal wisdom. Myths or fairy tales often have similarities among cultures, and these similarities are shown through their universal symbols and themes. Sometimes our own dreams may contain these kinds of symbols.

Of course, not all the symbols and images in our dreams represent the universal or archetypal. Many, if not most, are best interpreted by discovering the personal associations one has with that person or object. The dream symbol of a gun, for example, would likely mean one thing to a sportsman and something quite different to a victim of a shooting.

There is really no such thing as a bad dream because all dreams have the potential of helping the dreamer. Dreams of disastrous events may simply be advice telling us to change our diets or our attitudes, or they may be emotional releases from the various situations in our lives. They can become invaluable tools of instruction and guidance if we will only begin to work with them.

For example, one person who dreamed of a headless man in uniform was told in his Cayce reading that, instead of losing his head over his duties by following the letter of the law and getting too caught up in his job, there was a greater lesson to be learned by following the spirit of the law (137-36). A woman who dreamed of a wild man running through the streets, shouting and causing a great deal of trouble, was told that the dream was advice for her to control her temper (136-18). One lady dreamed that a friend of hers was speaking to her. She noticed that the woman had beautiful false teeth of different shapes, but every other tooth had the appearance of pure gold. She was told that the gold teeth represented the spiritual truths of which she herself was often speaking, but they were false because she had not applied them in her own life (288-14). Another woman dreamed that her mother, who had died, was alive and happy. Cayce assured her that she was not trying to fool herself, that her mother was indeed alive and happy, "for there is no death, only the transition from the physical to the spiritual plane" (136-33).

When we are trying to arrive at a dream interpretation, one possibility to consider is that the dream is largely literal. For example, seeing one's self eat a salad in a dream may simply indicate the need for a change in diet and eating more salads. We may dream of someone we have not heard from in a very long while and then meet that person a short time later. In other cases, the action may be much more symbolic of what is happening in waking life. Dreaming about different rooms that we have not yet explored could be pointing to the unopened doors of our own personality. A car can symbolize our physical body, it might be associated with our personal life's direction, or it could literally be a dream about our car.

Dreams of birth and death are often symbolic of new beginnings and, perhaps, the end of doing things the old way. In other words, a dreamed "death" may refer to the end of a part of our personality. For example, a woman who dreamed of attending the funeral of her minister's wife might be allowing the spiritual aspects of her own life to be overlooked or "laid to rest." Dreams of being pregnant or taking care of a small child who really does not exist in waking life is not necessarily a prediction (although it could be!); the dream might merely be pointing out a new condition that will be coming our way or a new idea to which we will soon give birth.

When dreams give guidance or seem to pass judgments, it is usually in response to values and ideals we have previously set for ourselves. Most dreams can be seen as a kind of comparison—Cayce used the word *correlation*. While we sleep, a comparison is made between recent actions and the inner values we hold. In a contemporary example, one woman was advised for health reasons to avoid eating chocolate, and yet she continued to eat it anyway. She had a dream in which she was crossing the border into Mexico illegally for the purpose of buying chocolate. Obviously, she was the best one to determine that her dream was simply pointing out that she was doing something she had been told not to do; at one level, she knew it was "illegal."

Scientific studies have shown that each of us dreams, but not all of us remember them. If you would like to try working with your dreams, you need to begin keeping a notepad by the bedside so that you can jot down whatever you remember immediately after waking up—even if it's only a feeling. If you get enough sleep, if you expect to start remembering your dreams, and if you make an effort to record whatever is on your mind when you awaken, you should be able to start remembering your dreams in a relatively short period of time. As you look at what's going on in your life and then look at a particular dream, you'll begin to have an idea of what individual symbols may mean to you—especially if the symbol repeats itself in later dreams. The symbol won't necessarily mean the same to you as to someone else because dreams are as individual as dreamers.

There is a simple, five-step approach to working with dreams that even the novice can begin using immediately:

1. Write down your dreams each day. Even if you remember only fragments, write them down.

2. Begin by realizing that the feeling you had about the dream is at least as important as trying to come up with any interpretation; besides, because of the multiple levels of our beings, dreams often have more than one meaning.

3. Remember that—for the most part—every character in the dream represents a part of yourself. Watch the actions, feelings, expressions, and conversations of these characters in your dreams and measure them against activities in your waking life.

4. Watch for recurring symbols, characters, and emotions in your dreams, and begin a personal "dream dictionary" of these symbols and what their importance may be to you.

5. When working with dreams, first remember that your dreams can be extremely helpful even if you don't recognize immediately what they mean; and, second, remember to practice, practice, practice!

The Cayce readings essentially classify dreams into three distinct categories: (1) dreams that relate to an individual's physical body and health; (2) dreams that address psychological issues or provide insights into understanding self; and (3) dreams that explore higher realms of consciousness, the spiritual nature of the soul, past lives, and even one's unfolding future.

In terms of a physical dream, on one occasion Edgar Cayce had been feeling tired and complaining of mental lethargy. He had a dream in which he looked inside his head and saw a motorized wheel that had stopped turning because a piece of trash had gotten in the way. In interpreting the dream, Cayce explained that the image illustrated a problem he was then having with eliminations (e.g., the trash), which was leading to his exhaustion and mental lethargy (294-56).

Often challenged by a lack of finances and the psychological worries of providing for his family, during one period Edgar Cayce had been particularly concerned about his financial situation. During that time he had a dream in which he was in Paris with the Duke and Duchess of Windsor and Jesus. The Windsors and Paris could be associated with wealth, and Jesus is certainly a symbol for spirituality. During their time together in Paris, Edgar Cayce realized he was without money—having only three cents in his pocket. Realizing the impoverished situation that Cayce was in, Jesus threw his head back and laughed aloud, clapped his hands together, and said: "Will I have to send YOU after a fish too?" Obviously a reference to Matthew 17:24–27, the dream was simply an encouragement to have faith in spite of the appearance of things (294-186).

A unique concept in the readings dealing with dreams is that Cayce suggested that nothing of significance ever happens to anyone without it first being foreshadowed in a dream! As an example, in October 1926, Gertrude Cayce had a dream in which she was crying because her family had been forced to move into a very tiny cottage that was too small for them. A reading was given on the dream in which Cayce stated it was "a forecast of conditions as will arise..." (538-22). The family thought nothing more of the dream until June 1931, nearly five years later, when backing was withdrawn from the Cayce hospital and they were evicted and forced to take up residency in a very small cottage.

Dreams can show us the desires that have been motivating us, and they can help us sense the needs of our bodies. They can provide insights for living life more creatively and assist us in making important decisions based on what we already know at a conscious level. For example, dreams may give us guidance on helping to heal a relationship, but only if we've already tried to do the best we can with that person. When we set our sights and make the decisions that are called for, then dreams will aid us by bringing life into clearer focus. Working with our dreams can be like speaking with a trusted friend who knows everything about us and is just there for us to discuss what's going on in our lives. Most of the time, the friend will just listen, but in the listening, we can begin to find the answers within ourselves. Although the answers may have been there all the time, we just never knew how to look for them.

Essentially, the purpose of dreams is to make us more consciously aware of what we are going through in our lives, based upon our thoughts, feelings, and actions. The Edgar Cayce information suggests that oftentimes dreams "contrast" and "correlate" the events of the day—giving us, perhaps, another way of looking at the experiences and relationships occurring in our lives.

THE READINGS' APPROACH TO ESP AND PSYCHIC PHENOMENA

Most individuals are familiar with *extrasensory perception* (ESP)—the ability to communicate or to receive information without the aid of one of the five known senses (taste, smell, hearing, touch, and sight). Rather than simply combining all psychic experiences into the same category, this extended ability to perceive can also be further refined and classified. Those categories most frequently demonstrated within Cayce's readings include *telepathy, clairvoyance, precognition*, and *retrocognition*.

Telepathy is also known as mind-to-mind communication. This is the ability to obtain information psychically by reading the mind of another person. When we suddenly start thinking about someone we have not heard from in a while and, a short while later, the phone rings and that other person is on the line, this is one example of telepathy.

Once, while giving a physical reading, Edgar Cayce spoke several sentences and a series of words. Meanwhile, his stenographer, Gladys Davis, sitting across the room, was wondering how the information should be punctuated. As if in response to her unspoken query, the unconscious Cayce told her to put commas between the words *body soul entity*. He went on to describe where a new paragraph should begin, as well as where she needed to place a set of parentheses. All this was evidence of telepathy because Gladys had simply thought of a question, and it was answered without ever being asked (531-2). It was an ability Cayce demonstrated on a number of occasions.

A second category of ESP is clairvoyance. Clairvoyance literally means "clear seeing," but it can also be used to suggest the ability to obtain information, sensations, sounds, and even smells through other than the physical senses. When a person perceives information in this manner, it does not necessarily come from another individual. For example, suppose you shuffled a deck of cards, placed them facedown, and then went through the deck and tried to name each one. If your percentage of correct guesses went far beyond what could be expected by random chance, it would be an example of clairvoyance—seeing the current order of the cards from the cards themselves. On the other hand, if you tried the same experiment with a friend who carefully looked at each card and concentrated on a card before you guessed, this could be an example of telepathy—reading the mind of your friend who saw each card. Although this example is pretty straightforward, for some of the case histories in the Cayce files it is difficult to determine whether telepathy or clairvoyance was most in operation.

Repeatedly, the Cayce readings demonstrated examples of clairvoyance that were later documented. Perhaps two of the most unusual are readings 373-1 and 4591-1. In both cases, Cayce was able to speak in foreign languages of which he had no conscious knowledge. In the first, given to a fifty-three-year-old man who had been born in Germany, Cayce merely spoke a couple of German sentences. However, in the other, Cayce gave the entire reading in Italian! A local Italian vendor was quickly summoned to take down the information in English. The request for the reading had been sent in by a man from Palermo, Sicily.

Clairvoyance may also have been demonstrated in an early reading given in 1907 (740-1). An attorney in New York wished to have evidence of Cayce's talent by being psychically "tracked" during the course of one day—at the time, Cayce was living in Kentucky. As soon as Cayce began the reading, he mentioned the time difference between the two cities—evidently, this was the first time he realized that Bowling Green, Kentucky, and New York, New York, were not in the same time zone. During the course of the reading,

Cayce described the man's activities. He "saw" the man enter a cigar store. While inside, the man smoked a cigarette and bought a certain brand of cigars. Afterward, the man went up the street to his office and, instead of waiting for the elevator (the reading said, "We will have him walk up so he will remember it"), he walked up the steps, and Cayce "heard" him whistling a certain song ("Annie Laurie"). In his office the attorney found a man waiting for him who wanted to discuss a piece of property at the end of the Williams Street Bridge. He turned to his desk and found three letters: a bill, a business letter, and a note from his girlfriend. Cayce then mentioned that the man had a meeting later in the day with a gentleman named "Dolligan." This information was all wired by telegram to Mr. [740] in New York. After several days, Cayce received a reply that read, in part:

> Your "reading" as to myself was correct in the main. As a matter of fact at the first hour named in your reading I was engaged in preparing papers in a matter for a client residing in Brooklyn. It had to do with an estate of a deceased person, all of which matters are transacted in the Surrogates Court situation situated in the New Hall of Records, which is only a short step from the Brooklyn Bridge connecting New York City and Brooklyn. I did have an engagement for this afternoon to go over a matter with Mr. Downey (not Dolligan), your telegram reaching me two or three hours before that conference was to take place...

Precognition—the ability to see into the future—is a third category of ESP evidenced in the readings. To a New York businessman interested in investments in the 1920s, Cayce advised the purchase of securities in the communications industries, stating that radio, and then telephone, communications would one day encircle the globe (257-36). In March 1929, six months before the stock market crash, reading 900-425 provided a New York stockbroker with a severe warning of the impending "great disturbance in financial circles." For many children, Cayce foresaw what they would be like as adults, even going so far as to describe hidden talents and occupational decisions. In 1941, eight months before the United States had even entered World War II, the readings predicted the arrival of peace in " '45 and '46" (270-47).

Precognition may have been evident in a reading given on January 18, 1925. At the time of the reading, Edgar Cayce lived in Dayton but was on a business trip in New York. He had just completed giving a reading for another case (4599-1) when he began talking about a Mrs. [5700] in Eugene, Missouri, who needed assistance. No one in the room knew why the information was being given, but it was written down by the stenographer. The reading said, in part:

Now, in this condition that has arisen in the body from the dis-arrangement in the pelvic organs, especially those in the false pelvis, we find these need attention at once, through that condition as given, for the operation on the body, else there will be in 19 days the setting up of an infection that will bring destructive forces to the whole system. The alleviation of the pressure has been effective to the body, but this attempt to lift that heavier than the body should have attempted, under the existing conditions, has brought about this condition, or falling more of the organs in the pelvis, and the rupture of the left Fallopian Tube, and these conditions should be attended to at once. 5700-6

Amazingly, when the Cayce family returned to Dayton several days later, they found a letter from the Missouri woman asking for assistance. Even without knowing about her request for information, all of her questions had been answered in the voluntary reading. In addition to the fact that Cayce did not receive the request for help until he returned home, it was later determined that [5700]'s letter may even have been written after the reading was given!

The Cayce files are filled with thousands of examples of retrocognition, which is a fourth major category of ESP. In simplest terms, retrocognition is the ability to see into the past. This enabled the readings to zero in on childhood experiences or trauma, the root cause of an illness or a fear, even ancient civilizations and past lives. Although much of the retrocognitive information may be impossible to verify—especially that which deals with the ancient past—repeatedly Cayce provided insights into history that have later proven accurate. For example, more than eleven years before the Dead Sea Scrolls were found in 1947, Edgar Cayce provided a great deal of information on a Jewish sect called the Essenes. He claimed that, in the Essene society, men and women lived and worked together. Scholars, however, believed that the Essenes were a monastic society composed exclusively of men. It was not until archaeological excavations occurred after Cayce's death that the psychic information was verified.

Some of the retrocognitive material deals with the much more recent past and is easier to validate. For example, in reading 1462-1, Edgar Cayce correctly gave the birthplace and date of a young woman for whom he was giving a reading, even though he had been mistakenly provided with the incorrect city and date of birth. On a number of occasions when individuals were seeking dream interpretation readings, such as 900-69, Cayce reminded the dreamer of forgotten portions of his or her own dream!

The case of Aimee Dietrich, one of the most celebrated of Cayce's early career, shows how retrocognition pinpointed the cause of her mental dysfunction and physical convulsions to a fall and an illness she had experienced at the age of two (2473-1). The girl had been to specialists for years, but no treatment had proven effective. Her father's affidavit from October 1910 stated in part: "She was now six years old and getting worse, had as many as twenty convulsions in one day, her mind was a blank, all reasoning power was entirely gone."

The reading provided a last-chance course of treatment that was followed. The father's affidavit continued:

> ...he went into a sleep or trance and diagnosed her case as one of congestion at base of the brain, stating also minor details. He outlined to Dr. A. C. Layne [Al C. Layne, D.O.], now of Griffin, Georgia, how to proceed to cure her. Dr. Layne treated her accordingly, every day for three weeks, using Mr. Cayce occasionally to follow up the treatment, as results developed. Her mind began to clear up about the eighth day and within three months she was in perfect health, and is so to this day. This case can be verified by many of the best citizens of Hopkinsville, Kentucky...
>
> *Signed—C. H. Dietrich*

Later, Aimee graduated with honors from the University of Kentucky. Unfortunately, as the years passed, the Dietrich and Cayce families moved and were no longer in touch with one another. Eventually, follow-up reports were obtained revealing that Aimee had contracted tuberculosis and died in 1934 at the age of thirty-seven.

These are just a few of the many examples of ESP in the Cayce readings. Cayce claimed that everyone is psychic to some degree because psychic activity is a natural ability of the soul. In fact, this idea perhaps best defines the readings' approach to psychic ability. Because "psychic is of the soul," the Cayce information suggested that it is relatively easy to induce personal psychic experiences. However, the readings advised that, instead of seeking psychic experiences for the sake of having them, we should seek only those within the context of spiritual growth, of learning about ourselves, or of being of service to others.

Another situation that occurs when dealing with psychic information is that people often have the tendency to make psychic experiences seem unusual, out of the ordinary, special, somehow set apart, or, perhaps, even frightening. However, in the Cayce approach, psychic information is as natural as intuition or having a hunch. In addition, just because something is psychic does not mean it's 100 percent accurate. We may wish to work with psychic information to the same degree that we would listen to the advice of a trusted friend. It can be utilized as an additional tool for gathering insights and for making decisions. It should not necessarily be given any more credence than information from any of our other friends or senses; however, it should not be given any less either. In time, people may work with their intuition in such a way that it becomes as natural as using any of their other senses.

Whether it's telepathy, clairvoyance, precognition, or retrocognition, the Edgar Cayce material provides an impressive collection of documented case histories for further investigation, research, and inquiry. In fact, what may be unique about the more than fourteen thousand recorded readings given by Edgar Cayce is the attending documentation. Every stenographic transcript includes more than simply the reading itself: It includes also the names of all individuals present, the location, time, date, and other pertinent information. In addition to background reports explaining why the person was asking specific information or how he or she found out about Cayce, there are accompanying reports, letters, and follow-up corroboration. This meticulous attention to detail makes it possible to state with complete certainty that Edgar Cayce remains the most carefully witnessed, investigated, and documented psychic of all time.

THE READINGS' APPROACH
TO SPIRITUAL GROWTH

One of the major concepts in the readings is that the purpose of life is primarily for soul growth and personal transformation. For this reason, over an eleven-year period between 1931 and 1942, Edgar Cayce gave a series of one hundred thirty readings to a group of people in Norfolk, Study Group #1, who asked questions about the practicality of working with spiritual laws on Earth. Interestingly enough, some members of the group had originally been interested in obtaining information on how to become more psychic. Cayce responded that the goal was rather to become more spiritual and that, as individuals worked more consistently with spiritual principles, they would naturally become more psychic.

The material provided by Edgar Cayce was eventually compiled by the first study group into a collection of essays on spiritual lessons and was later published as *A Search for God, Books I and II.* Over the years, this series of readings on spiritual growth has guided and enabled people from every religious background to become more aware of themselves and their relationship to one another. Small, interdenominational study groups exist worldwide, exploring the readings' approach to cooperation, service, love, meditation, and prayer.

From Cayce's perspective, we are essentially spiritual beings who are having a physical experience. Unfortunately, too often we become focused on the material things in life rather than upon our true spiritual heritage. One of the readings states:

> ... Thou shalt love the Lord thy God with all thine heart, thy neighbor *as* thyself! This [is] the whole law, this [is] the whole answer to the world, to each and every soul. That is the answer to the world conditions as they exist today ...

> Man's answer to everything has been *Power*—Power of money, Power of position, Power of wealth, Power of this, that or the other. This has *never* been *God's* way, will never be God's way. Rather little by little, line upon line, here a little, there a little, each thinking rather of the other ... 3976-8

With this in mind, Cayce often told people that their goal in life should be to make "the world a better place because ye have lived in it" (5249-1 and others).

THE INEVITABLE DESTINY of every soul is to become cognizant of its true individuality while maintaining an awareness of its oneness with God. For all of humankind, this state of enlightenment is seemingly achievable in one of two ways: either by learning the lesson of unconditional love and then moving on to other stages of consciousness development or by literally attaining perfection on Earth.

From Cayce's perspective, the purpose of life is to become a better channel through which the Creator can manifest on Earth. In fact, this ability to become a light to others and a channel through which God can operate in the material world is the rationale behind all of the information on soul growth contained in the Cayce files. Since our ultimate purpose here on Earth is to come to know our true relationship with God, the readings frequently recommended meditation—a key to truly understanding that relationship.

Cayce began recommending meditation as early as 1921, long before most people even knew what it was. Many people began hearing about meditation during the 1960s and 1970s. At first, they might have thought it was something unusual or even bizarre or else something done only in Eastern religions. However, a great deal of clinical research has proven that meditation can positively affect our health and well-being. By practicing this method of becoming silent, people can reduce their anxiety levels and learn to become more relaxed. Many physicians now recommend meditation as an effective way for patients to lower their blood pressure.

In simplest terms, meditation is the practice of quieting our physical bodies and minds and focusing our attention inward instead of upon the outside world. It promotes coordination at three levels: physically, we begin to relax; mentally, our busied thoughts become quiet; and spiritually, we become reenergized and more capable of dealing lovingly and effectively with the people and events around us. As we take the time each day to put away from our thoughts the countless cares with which we are bombarded, we can begin to reestablish an awareness of our own spiritual nature. In one respect, prayer is talking to God, but meditation is listening to that portion of our being which is in constant communion with the Divine.

In addition to meditation, the readings encouraged individuals to work with personal application and spiritual ideals in their daily lives. With persistent application and attunement, true personal transformation and soul growth result. In addition to people transforming themselves one at a time, Cayce believed that only this approach would ultimately lead to the transformation of the world and to lasting peace on Earth.

WHAT IS MOST exciting about the Cayce readings is their internal consistency. When the more than fourteen thousand readings are taken as a whole, there is a wealth of material on medicine, history, life after death, dreams, psychic ability, attitudes and emotions, child rearing, diet, and relationships, providing helpful insights into nearly any topic imaginable.

It is interesting to note that in the forty-three years during which the readings were given, Cayce never heard a word he said in the sleep state; nor did he remember anything when he awoke. To understand the nature of his own Work, he spent many long hours poring over the information in the readings that had been written down by his secretary. His story is really that of a humble man who went on to become one of the most helpful psychics the world has ever known. The information in the readings, available to us today, became his gift to the world.

CHAPTER 3

EXAMPLES OF TELEPATHY AND CLAIRVOYANCE

Edgar Cayce's demonstration of his uncanny psychic ability when he gave a reading was preceded by putting himself into a self-induced trance. For each reading, he would lie down on a couch, become comfortable, put his hands up to his forehead, and begin to pray. When he saw a brilliant flash of light, it was the signal that he could continue. He would lower his hands to his stomach, and when his eyelids began to flutter, the conductor (most often his wife) would give him the appropriate suggestion. In this state, it seemed that he could answer any question or provide any type of information requested.

Often he would begin speaking as though he could see specific details of what was occurring around the person for whom he was giving the reading at that very moment in time. Even though the person might be hundreds of miles away, Cayce spoke as though that person was in the same room. Here are examples of this activity and the follow-up reports:

> Gertrude Cayce: You will go over this body carefully, examine it thoroughly and tell me the conditions you find at the present time, giving the cause of the existing conditions, also suggestions for help and relief of this body; answering the questions as I ask them.

> Edgar Cayce: Yes, not bad-looking pajamas!

> We have the body here [subject in California]. As we find, there are disturbing conditions. There has been in the body, for some time back, conditions wherein the tautness in the bronchi and trachea, with the taxation of the muscular and nerve forces, has produced weaknesses and allergies...5196-1

> Mr. [5196]'s letter: "In answer to your letter inquiring for a report on the Physical Reading given for me...Yes, I deliberately donned a pair of new pajamas of a bright color. The diagnosis was the same as several chiropractors had given me before and several after..." 5196-1 Reports

> Edgar Cayce: Yes, we have the body here, [549], Millinery Department [in Tennessee]...now waiting on a lady in front of a glass with knot on posts—two sit together, you see—on the back one. Yes, quite an interesting lady, though, she is waiting on; she needs a reading, too! to take

this knot off of her! As we find with this body, [549], there are those conditions that disturb the better physical functioning of the body. These, as we find, affect the digestive system as well as the general circulation, and are of the natures that affect the tissue in portions of the body; especially in the lower pelvic organs, making reflex conditions through the nerve systems...549-1

Miss [243]'s letter: "Mrs. [542] and Miss [549] are both so happy with their readings...they are both taking treatments from the same osteopath, Dr. Watson—a woman, and they say she was delighted with the diagnosis and is treating by the reading. Miss [549]'s was funny, wasn't it, when it started off? She is a designer and said she was helping Mrs. Miller with a hat. She said she thought Mrs. Miller would get a reading."

Miss [549]'s letter: "The reading is splendid and I wish to say I do feel greatly relieved. I am taking the osteopathic treatment; at present I have had five treatments...I do really feel much better, although I still have a little aching in the lower part of my body...549-1 Reports

Hugh Lynn Cayce: You will give the physical condition of this body at the present time [located in Pennsylvania], with suggestions for further corrective measures; answering the questions she submits, as I ask them:

Edgar Cayce: [When locating the street and number]—
That's a right pretty tree on the corner!

Yes; we have the body here, [1100]; this we have had
before.

As we find, the general physical forces of the body are
very good—in the present. 1100-27

Mrs. [1100]'s letter: "Thank you so much for the readings
and your dear letter.

"Yes, there is an unusually lovely tree on the corner of
our apartment building. The building is four stories high
and the tree is slightly taller." 1100-27 Reports

[Physical suggestion given]

Edgar Cayce: Yes—982 [repeating address]—That's a
very nice place! [Subject in Florida.]

We have the body, [1100]; this we have had before.

Improvements are still indicated in the body, and as
we find if there are the precautions taken, not too soon
beginning to overtax the body, the body should continue
to be on the improve. 1100-14

Mrs. [1100]'s letter: "The reading came yesterday and I
want to thank you very much.

"I was quite amused when the information said, 'A very
nice place,' because it is just that and the people here are
lovely...Clearwater is very small but quite pretty and this

hotel is unusually nice. Lounge rooms and sun porches galore, also a beautiful roof on which I can take sun baths after I get stronger. Am trying to take it slowly, as I know too much sun is very bad, especially when one still runs a bit of temperature. Know that will be leaving me shortly...Am trying very hard to 'work at the play and play at the work of getting well.' Thank you so much." 1100-14 Reports

[Physical suggestion given]

Edgar Cayce: 1075 Park Avenue, Apt. 80...very unusual in some of these halls, isn't it—what funny paintings!

Yes—we have the body here, [3904]...3904-1

From [3904]: "Dr. found spinal condition to exist, just as described by Mr. Cayce. Treated accordingly several months...

"Osteopathy, with special attention to 3rd and 4th lumbar centers...

"[Regarding the 'funny paintings'] Yes—include wood plaques from Central America and other unusual wall adornments." 3904-1 Reports

Gertrude Cayce: You will have before you the body and enquiring mind of [930], located at...34th Street [subject in New York], who seeks information, advice and guidance as to his mental and material welfare. You will answer the questions he has submitted, as I ask them.

Edgar Cayce: Yes (he's on his way), we have the enquiring mind, [930]…930-1

Letter from [257]: "It was very wonderful on the reading for [930]—that he was on the bus at 3:20 and was late at Dr. […]'s office—but you said he was enroute and he was. He requires a lot of help…You will be able to help him also in his decision of the new position…" 930-1 Reports

Letter from [930]: "At the appointed time of the reading I was unfortunately delayed, while enroute started to concentrate, offered up my prayer to the Almighty to give me guidance through you…" 930-1 Reports

Edgar Cayce's psychic prowess with telepathy, or mind-to-mind communication, is certainly evident in each of these cases, but most often the information received in his readings goes far beyond simple mind reading. In thousands of cases, with no more information than merely a name and address, Cayce described exact symptoms, named specific ailments, and then outlined detailed regimens of treatment.

On November 12, 1943, an interesting reading presented itself. Edgar Cayce had nearly finished giving three readings for people who had written to him for help ([3368], [3498], and [2390]). Unbeknownst to Cayce's wife, Gertrude, who was conducting the readings, or his stenographer, Gladys, who was taking down the information, in another part of the house

Harmon Bro, a member of the office staff, was speaking on the phone to a woman in Charlottesville, Virginia, who was extremely upset. Her daughter [308], who had received readings from Cayce in the past, had fallen out of a bunk bed at college and possibly injured her spine. Unable to walk, the girl had been confined to the infirmary at the College of William and Mary, in Williamsburg, Virginia.

When the three assigned readings for the day had been completed, rather than waking up, the sleeping Cayce continued speaking and volunteered the following information:

Now we have those conditions that exist with [308] . . . [in an undertone] Charlottesville—Williamsburg. These are bruises, though the structural portions also are bruised.

Apply Glyco-Thymoline Packs in those areas, as on hips and the spine, as well as in the 3rd cervical center. Then apply heat, not with an electric pad but with heavy salt heated in pads or bags. This will remove the strain as well as alkalize the drainages that must necessarily be set up by the use at this particular time of a senna base laxative, such as Dr. Caldwell's Syrup of Pepsin. This would be good for the body.

Keep the Glyco-Thymoline Packs. Change them about every three to four hours. Keep them on for about the same length of time and then leave off, but next day use them again—until this soreness disappears.

After tomorrow, begin to set up drainages by massage.

This means the fourteenth, you see. After tomorrow begin with the massage. Yes, this is the twelfth—we haven't made a mistake! We are through. 308-12

Neither Gladys nor Gertrude understood why the information had been given, but it was taken down nonetheless. Later that same day, the incident was discussed with Harmon Bro, who had been on the phone. Suddenly everything made sense. A follow-up report from the girl's mother is on file:

"My daughter, [308], was trying to get in bed—the top side of a double decker, at William and Mary College. She slipped on the chair and hit the end of her spine. By the next morning she couldn't get out of bed and was taken to the infirmary. Her roommate called me about 10 a.m., on 11/12/43. I then received a call from the doctor at the infirmary and he wanted to know if I wanted some X-rays made; I told him I would let him know. Then I phoned Mr. Cayce's home and talked with Harmon Bro, who explained that so many readings were scheduled that he didn't think [308]'s could be gotten in today—it was too late to mention it to Mr. Cayce since he had already started the check physical readings for the morning, but he would tell him later.

"I was so confused that I prayed constantly for guidance. At 9 p.m. that night I phoned Gladys and asked her how long she thought it would be before a check reading could be gotten. She said, 'We got it—it came through at the end of the other readings, without the suggestion being given to obtain it!'

"...Evidently my anxiety in Charlottesville had gotten through to him...

"We followed the treatments for three days and she returned to school. She has never had any trouble since."
308-12 Reports

The files within the vault of the Edgar Cayce Foundation are filled with testimonials and follow-up confirmations, not only from the patients themselves but also from doctors, health-care professionals, and various researchers. All of this information is open to the public and available for personal research and investigation. These testimonies, reports, even X-ray corroboration provide subsequent confirmation of Cayce's diagnoses as well as the effectiveness of his prescribed treatments.

In case 551-1, a reading was requested by a young man in New York City who had made no comment about his condition. After the reading, a doctor confirmed the information that was provided from the trance state. Here is a portion of the reading, along with the attending documentation:

Edgar Cayce:...These conditions, as we find, have to do with certain centers in the nerve system that are impinged in such manner as to prevent the circulation, especially in the eliminating and incentive receiving centers, causing an unequalized amount of dross or refuse to accumulate in various portions of the body, forming self then in to that mass or condition in tissue and fibre of the system known as catarrhal conditions, such as exist in the inner ear, nose, intestines, in stomach proper. These all then, at various times, show the excess of this condition forming in the system. The radiations from these centers, then, which are depressed, as we find come from the 12th, 11th, 10th dorsal and in the 5th and 4th cervicals. These affect then the circulation as directed from these portions and prevent the tissue receiving the incentive to produce perfect eliminations in the system. We have this excess created, as we find, after there has been especial nerve tension, or an excess of foods with the body under nerve tension. The body becomes easily irritated under such conditions, having what would be termed blue or gloomy days, to which the mind, the whole system, seems to submerge at such times. These, then, are symptoms. These, then, are the conditions in physical to which the body should be warned, or from which take warning.

To remove those conditions, and to bring the body where the physical may function normally and nominally, would be to first have these subluxations removed by manipulation, osteopathically preferably given, in these regions as given, and so stimulate by heat (any vibration may be used; Alpine Ray, Violet ray, Radial ray. Any that stimulate nerve and blood secretion through parts that have been subluxated), and with this stimulus we will find the body would respond readily through physical forces. These, then, would be necessary three to five treatments, taken one every other day, until the system is in its normal position, condition. Then it will be necessary only to take them once a month, or such a matter, or when necessary for the body to gain its physical, mental, equilibrium ... 551-1

Letter from Mr. [551]: "This is in reference to your reading of the 12th [and] instructions concerning my health and business success.

"Following your instructions I have placed myself under the care of an able osteopath, Dr. Joseph Ferguson ... who has found by his examinations your reading correct in every detail, except a few minor defects which are now being treated in conjunction with your given suggestions. This afternoon was my fifth treatment ..." 551-1 Reports

Letter from attending physician: "Dear Mr. Cayce: I take pleasure in reporting to you regarding the case of Mr. [551] who consulted me on March 17th, following your report to him on his physical condition.

"I found the cervical and lower dorsal subluxations which you mentioned and also the third, fourth and fifth dorsals were somewhat anterior. Mr. [551] is having these mechanical conditions corrected and they have already shown considerable improvement. I am raying him with the Ultra-Violet Ray by means of the Alpine Lamp, which is the name given to the air cooled, mercury quartz lamp made by The Hanovia Chemical Co., of Newark, N.J. . . .

"Mr. [551] is resting much better and shows considerable improvement in every way. Yours respectfully, Joseph Ferguson, D.O." 551-1 Reports

In another instance, a Norfolk man [556] was taken violently ill one June evening. Neither he, his wife, nor their physician could figure out what was wrong until after Cayce's diagnosis. His wife later reported:

"He went for a walk. . . and was brought home by a friend. He was suffering severe pain in the head, and vomited quantities of blood. The next day, I called an Osteopath and a physician to try to determine the cause of the condition. The physician believed it was either a sinus or perhaps an abscessed tooth, and advised him to consult his dentist. I 'phoned our dentist who came, and stated the condition was not from his teeth. By this time, he was suffering excruciating pain, and his head and face were swelling. The dentist suggested that I call a specialist. [My husband] protested against such a procedure, and begged me to allow no one to touch his head or mouth. I sat a moment in deliberation, and. . . it was then, Mr. Cayce came to my mind. I called on the 'phone, and Miss Gladys answered. I said, 'Mr. [556] is seriously ill; ask Mr. Cayce if he will give a reading. I want to know one thing, where is the source of infection?' I gave no description of his condition, nor any of the symptoms…the doctors did not know what was causing the illness." 556-5 Reports

An emergency reading was requested. While the man remained in Norfolk, twenty miles away in Virginia Beach, Edgar Cayce was able to describe the problem:

…there is a closing—as it were—in the area of the emptying of the stomach in the duodenum. And this causes those portions where there is some bloating or swelling; great pains through the abdominal area, through even the face and those portions where the connections are with same…

The wife's report continued:

"Lengthy details were given as to course of treatment, all of which I followed to the letter, calling for additional advice from time to time, and following each of them closely. He had lost weight very fast, and by October had gained back all of it. By November he was restored to normal health.

"Words fail me to express to you, and to the world, the wonderful merits of the information that comes through the Readings. Scientifically speaking, a condition of this kind is seldom overcome without an operation, and then taking a patient from 12 to 18 months to recover therefrom."

A questionnaire completed by the family physician contained the following report:

(1) Did the Reading presented to you describe the condition of the patient?
(A) Yes. I confirmed it with the "Pathodast Blood Testing" instrument.

(2) Were the suggestions for your treatment in your opinion proper for this condition?
(A) Yes.

(3) For what period of time has the patient followed directions given in the Reading under your care?
(A) The full time.

(4) What results have you observed?
(A) Excellent.

(5) Comment.
(A) The specific infections were streptococci, colisepsis, acidosis and general anemia.

Signed—Dr. Carl S. Frischkorn

Not unexpectedly, the doctors to whom patients went in order to follow the treatments outlined in the readings often insisted on obtaining their own diagnosis. In the case of 565-1, the woman had been in extremely poor health for approximately eight or nine years. Her symptoms included pains in the top of the head, dizziness, lack of appetite, excess kidney activity, etc. Mrs. [565] took her reading to a new physician who refused to follow the advice until he had made his own diagnosis and checked her X-rays. To demonstrate the thoroughness of Cayce's clairvoyant insights, here is the majority of the reading she received:

[Cayce in Virginia, patient in North Carolina]

Edgar Cayce: Yes, we have the body here, [565].

Now, as we find, while there are many conditions physical with this body that are very good, there are those conditions that with the correction would make a much better body physically and mentally for the activities in the mental, spiritual and material body.

The disturbances, as we find, have to do with some minor conditions respecting functionings of organs, and little or no organic disorder. While many portions of the system are involved at one time or another, the conditions are such that they may be easily corrected in the present.

These, then, are conditions as we find them with this body, [565]:

First, in the blood supply, here we find the form of an anemia, or the lack of a proper balance in the numbers of the red blood cells and the white blood cells. This condition, while of an active nature, changes at times; for we may find at times there would be almost sufficient in numbers of the red and quite a deficiency in the white, while again we may find an alteration in just the opposite direction. This arises from nervous conditions that disturb the circulation, and the assimilation of that taken as food values for the body. The nerve disturbance arises, as we shall see, from two—yea, three—distinct causes, making a combination of disorders contributory—as will be seen—one to another. Hence there is not only the variation in the red and white blood supply, or the form of anemia, but the character of the disturbance in other portions of the body, as we shall see.

As to the characterization of the blood itself; that is, the hemoglobin, the urea, the activity in its coagulation and in the blood count; this varies, not so much as to cause what may be termed an unbalanced metabolism but the very character of the nervous condition makes low blood pressure and at times disturbances to the heart's activity and its pulsation. Dizziness arises at times from distinct causes, during the periods of the menstrual activity in elimination and during the periods when there is over exhaustion by excitement to the nerve forces of the body, or at other times we may find it arising purely from gases that form from nervous indigestion. These changes and alterations in the pressure cause changes in the character of the blood itself, though the body may not be said to have a blood disturbance—but the functioning of the organs themselves and their activity upon the system through the nerve supply makes the disturbance, though the character of the blood so far as carrying poisons or any character of bacilli in same is lacking; for it is very good in these directions.

In the nerve forces of the body we find much that is a cause, and much that is an effect. So, it is not altogether nerves; though the body is nervous naturally from those conditions that have existed and do exist in the body, but under stress or strain no one would call the body, [565], a nervous person; for she would be very quiet and very determined and very set in what she would do, and she would do it!

In the cerebro-spinal system we find there has been a relaxation in the 3rd and 4th dorsal area that has tended to make for a relaxing in the position of the stomach itself, or the organs or the nerve tendons and muscular forces through the hypogastric and pneumogastric plexus, as to allow the stomach itself to tilt to the lower side, or the pyloric end up and the hypogastric or the cardiac and lower than normal, you see. This makes for a tendency of easy fermentation in same, and is a natural strain on the nerve system. The muscular reactions cause the condition, but the effect is in the nerve system; and as those plexus in the upper dorsal are in close connection or association with the sympathetic and sensory nerve reactions through the ganglia near the 1st, 2nd and 3rd dorsal area, this makes for a slowing of the circulation to the head, you see, sympathetically. Hence organs of the sensory system sympathetically become involved, as at times there is the tendency for a quick drying of the throat—and the body feels like it would spit cotton often! At other times we have a thumping or drumming in the ear. At others there are the tendencies for the conditions to produce irritations and burnings in the eyes, especially if there has been an eyestrain either by being in the wind, poor light or strong light; any of these will produce an irritation through the necessary energies used and the lack of supply of nerve energy from the depletion in the area as indicated.

From this sympathetic condition, both as to the nerve supplies to the organs of digestion and as to the activities in the eliminations of the body during the periods that should be natural or normal, the reactions also produce an irritation again which causes the secretions from the vagina in such measures or manners as to make irritations so that the body is irritable in manner; and until the flow has begun there are pains produced in top of head, dizziness, lack of appetite, and an excess activity of the kidneys or bladder. These are purely reflex and are sympathetic conditions, as we have indicated, from a subluxation in the 3rd and 4th dorsal plexus area.

As to the activities of the organs themselves:

In the brain forces the reactions and activities are near normal.

The organs of the sensory system, as indicated, are disturbed through reflex conditions arising from the upper dorsal and reflexly through the cervical area.

Lungs, bronchi, larynx, only at periods when there are irritations to the hypogastric area is there any disorder of a nature not normal, but this will be corrected when the corrections are made throughout the system.

The digestive system, as indicated, shows disturbances; not only as to position of the stomach itself but as related to the digestive activities and reflexly to the heart's activity through poor circulation impoverished by the inactivity of that assimilated being properly directed in the system, and sympathetically also for the organs of the pelvis in their activity.

The liver, spleen, pancreas, as we find, would function near normal when there is a normalcy from the position or the activities of the body. When there are those changes that may be brought about by the addition of those properties necessary for creating a balance in the system, these will make for proper activity throughout the body.

Then, in making the corrections for this body, [565], we are speaking of:

First we would begin with making the proper adjustments osteopathically, especially—or specifically—in the upper dorsal area, *coordinating* the rest of the ganglia and the activity of the organs with same as these corrections are made. As we find, this would not require more than sixteen such adjustments and treatments.

Begin immediately, when the body rests, with having the feet very much higher than the head; and after such a rest there should be the holding of the stomach better in position by the use of bandage or belt about the body. Not so tight as to cause discomfort, but as the manipulations and adjustments are made let these be of *sufficient* activity as to *hold* the position of the stomach, that the activities through same may be kept in their proper relationship with the rest of the system.

For those disturbances that have been produced by the nerve reaction to the other organs of the system, so as to make that incentive for the corrections being made to coordinate with the activities of the glands and functioning of the organs, we would take a compound put together in this manner; adding the ingredients in the order named:

To 16 ounces of distilled water, we would add; stirring in; beating fine or powdering each ingredient:

Dried Wild Ginseng Root
(rolled together or beat very fine)   1 ounce
Indian Turnip   ½ dram
Wild Ginger (now this isn't Wild Ginseng,
but Ginger—which is a different root entirely)   1 dram

Boil slowly until it will amount to, when strained, 12 ounces. Then add to the solution 2 ounces pure grain alcohol and 1 ounce Syrup or Essence of Wild Cherry.

See? The dose would be ½ teaspoonful twice each day, morning on arising before the meal and when ready to retire. And continue taking until the whole quantity has been taken, you see.

Keep the manipulations about twice each week, making corrections specifically in the upper dorsal area and the *general* conditions throughout the body made to coordinate with same.

This would be an outline for the diet, though it may be altered as the seasons change, you see:

Mornings—citrus fruit or dry cereals with fruit or berries and milk, but do not use the citrus fruits and the cereals at the same meal, or quantities of milk with the citrus fruit. Very crisp bacon with browned bread, coddled egg or the like may be taken at the same meal. These may be altered at times to fresh fruits or stewed fruits, stewed rhubarb or the like, which are well but change them from time to time.

Noons—either a liquid diet or a green fresh-vegetable diet; such as juices of vegetables, juices of meats, but do not combine the green vegetables and the soups—or the liquid diet *with* the green or fresh vegetables. Include all the vegetables that may be eaten in a salad. And if there is to be taken any pastry, pie, cake, cream or the like, eat it at the noon meal—not in the evening or morning meals.

Evenings—preferably well-cooked vegetables, with at least one period each day (either morning or evening—and well that it be altered) of beef *juices*; not the meats but the beef juices made fresh every few days, not large quantities, but that we may change the activities in the system as to the correction in the blood supply. The meats should be rather those of fowl, liver, tripe, pigs' feet, or the like. Any of these should be included as to meats, but the greater portion should be of vegetables—with meats such as these taken at least three times each week.

Do these and, as we find, in thirty-six to forty days we will have a body quite a bit changed and near normal.

565-1

From a distance of more than 150 miles away, Edgar Cayce gave the woman a thorough examination (including X-rays!), discussed symptoms which had not been communicated to him, outlined a regimen of treatment that included physiotherapy, diet, and massage, and—in spite of her years of difficulty—provided reassurance that she could regain her health. Certainly, much more than telepathy is at work here. Mrs. [565] was so thrilled and encouraged by her reading that she told her sister she "wouldn't take $5 million dollars for it." Accompanying reports from the woman and her doctor are on file:

Letter from Mrs. [565]: "When the reading was received I was determined to carry it out to the letter if possible. I went to the Tucker-Carson Sanitarium in Raleigh, and the reading was turned over to Dr. Tucker. I asked him if he would treat me as suggested in the reading. After reading it he said he would not treat me as suggested, and would give me no treatment at all until after he had made a thorough examination, which I submitted to. I went to his office 4 days in succession. I was X-rayed several times and was given a very thorough examination. At the completion of this I was informed that his diagnosis of my case including the X-ray pictures were identical to the diagnosis in the reading, after which he treated me as suggested in the reading. I followed the diet as closely as possible and after several treatments I began to feel some improvements. I continued with the treatment and took every treatment as suggested in the reading. I can truthfully say that I feel better than I have felt in years. I can drive my car and go any place that I wish at any time, something I have not been able to do in years. I am indeed most grateful to you." 565-1 Reports

Letter from Dr. Tucker: "Mrs. [565] was under our care for about six weeks, her last treatment being July 31st, 1934. We made Gastrointestinal X-ray and checked her up physically for every angle. Your diagnosis was verified by our physical findings and we followed closely as possible your suggestions as to treatment. Mrs. [565] made splendid progress under treatment and she told me to-day that she is much better than she has been for a long time.

"I appreciate your referring Mrs. [565] to us and will be glad to co-operate with you in any case you send. We certainly appreciate your recommending the other three patients you mentioned in your letter, and if they come to us we will do our very best for them.

Sincerely, [Dr.] A. R. Tucker." 565-1 Reports

Nearly two-thirds of the readings deal with matters of health, covering every imaginable illness and disease that existed during Cayce's lifetime. His recommendations for treatment drew from every medical discipline and prescribed all manner of therapies, from diet, exercise, and physiotherapy, to prescription medication and even surgery. He was not a psychic healer; instead, he provided intuitive insights as to the nature of the illness and outlined a series of recommendations for the person to help that individual become well. Many of the recommendations needed to be carried out by a medical professional.

Although thousands of cases provided patients with hope and a specific regimen to follow, on occasion even the readings could not be optimistic. One example is the case of a sixty-nine-year-old man:

[Physical suggestion]
Edgar Cayce: Yes—quite serious.

Little may be offered as changes from those being administered in the present.

For, these—unless there is better coordination in the heart's activity—are close to separations [death].

Keep the body quiet...550-10

Later, Edgar Cayce received a newspaper clipping from the family announcing that the man had died the very next day.

On a few occasions, Cayce's psychic diagnosis could not be substantiated. An example is the case of a fifty-eight-year-old man with stomach ulcers as well as a tumor on his left arm. The reading described how a nervous shock had produced a detrimental reaction throughout his entire nervous system. However, the chief warning seemed to involve a blood condition. The reading stated, in part:

The blood is [in] an impoverished condition. There is a lack of the proper constituents to make the perfect distribution within the blood of the conditions found through the digestive track and the stomach itself. The effect upon the body is to reduce the vital forces within the body. The effect upon the circulation is to reduce the vital forces within the body.

There is insufficient hemoglobin of the nature which produces the carbon needed in the blood to take from the system the poisons created by the stomach and intestinal condition...13-1

After Mr. [13] received his reading, he went to a physician in order to confirm Cayce's diagnosis. The man's letter suggested that the reading was incorrect:

Letter from [13]: "I had my physician make a test of my blood and he says my blood is in fine condition—test 100%. He says my color is extra fine. Do you suppose a mistake was made...?" 13-1 Reports

Interestingly enough, fifteen years later the man died. According to the death certificate, the cause was "acute monocytic leukemia."

In case 3599-1, a woman had asked for a reading and stated that she could be found one and a half miles northeast of a certain highway. In giving the reading, Cayce corrected her and stated: "One and one half miles north-east—yes, it's one and five-eighths."

For a thirty-four-year-old deep-sea diver, the readings described the location of the *Lusitania*, provided a lengthy description of the ship's structural integrity upon the ocean floor, gave an estimated worth of the gold bullion still locked in the ship's strong room, and discussed the bodies that were still trapped within the wreckage (1395-1).

To an individual who was getting ready to leave the house in spite of the reading appointment time, Cayce said, "Come back here and sit down!" (3601-1).

After locating another individual for whom he was giving

a reading he said, ". . . they have had an accident right in front of the house" (599-10).

Whether it was psychic diagnosis or the ability to describe events as they occurred on the other side of a continent, the documentation in the Cayce files makes it clear that the readings were not bound by the confines of time and space. Somehow, while in the trance state, Edgar Cayce had access to information not consciously known to any other person. Whether the information came from the subconscious mind of the person for whom he was giving the reading or from some type of universal akashic record, it becomes apparent that his mind could be elevated to an almost limitless consciousness. It was an ability that frequently provided Edgar Cayce with an extended sense perception, even into the future.

CHAPTER 4

EXAMPLES OF PRECOGNITION

Although Edgar Cayce accurately predicted many events, he remained insistent that nothing that dealt with the future was fixed or destined; instead, because of the nature of free will and choice, the future was not unalterably written. For that reason, a number of people were given readings that presented distinct possibilities for their lives, depending upon how they exercised their own free wills. One of the most striking cases in this regard was given to the parents of an eleven-year-old boy, who were told that their son could become "a Jesse James" or "a Beethoven."

Edgar Cayce: Yes, we have the records here of that entity now known as or called [3633].

In giving the interpretations of the records here of this entity, it would be very easy to interpret same either in a very optimistic or a very pessimistic vein. For there are great possibilities and great obstacles. But know, in either case, the real lesson is within self. For here is the opportunity for an entity (while comparisons are odious, these would be good comparisons) to be either a Beethoven or a Whittier or a Jesse James or some such entity! For the entity is inclined to think more highly of himself than he ought to think, as would be indicated. That's what these three individuals did, in themselves. As to the application made of it, depends upon the individual self.

Here is an entity who has abilities and faculties latent within self which may be turned into music or poetry, or writing in prose, which few would ever excel. Or there may be the desire to have its own way to such an extent that the entity will be in the position to disregard others altogether in every form, just so self has its own way...

As to the abilities of the entity in the present, that to which it may attain and how:

There are unlimited abilities. How will they be directed by the entity? How well may others cause the entity to be aware of such activities? These should be the questions in self.

Study to know first thy ideals, spiritual, mental and material. Then apply self in such a manner towards those that there will never be a question mark after thine own conscience nor in the eyes even of others.

Remember that the Lord loveth the cheerful giver as well as those who seek His face.

Ready for questions.

(Q) What should be his chief work?

(A) This depends upon what he chooses—whether in music, directing of music, writing of music, or writing of verse. But in either of these channels, there may be the greater outlet. The voice of the wood, the voice of the air— any of those are the realms through which the entity may exceed, as well as succeed.

(Q) Should all of his talents be developed?

(A) All his talents will either be developed, or run to seed and be drained off. 3633-1

2/14/44 Letter from [3633]'s mother: "Your reading for [3633] was no surprise to my husband and me. We early saw that such tremendous energy should be set to work, and he is in his third year at a very strict, very religious boarding school. Idleness would destroy him. He must always be in the big world where he will be just a 'drop in the bucket'—not the 'big frog in a small pond'..."

9/49 Letter from [3633]'s mother: "We are in great distress now over the condition of our only child who has a distressing mental and nervous upset which as yet has not been diagnosed..."

3/7/51 Letter from [3633]'s mother: "The press has been cruel to us in our sorrow, and no doubt you have read of our tragedy. My son [3633], who has been emotionally unbalanced for 3 years, last Wednesday shot his father and grandmother. Hugh Lynn, your Father was my friend and I brought [3633] to see him and also he gave a life reading for him which had plenty of warnings in it. I am writing to ask you to please get one of your prayer circles to work on us— and to pour spiritual power into my mother [...] and into my husband [...] and my son [3633]. We certainly need it..."

4/26/51 Letter from [3633]'s mother: "Thanks so much for your letter about my son [3633]. In the light of our tragic happenings, your Father's reading for him takes on great significance..."

8/51 Letter from [3633]'s mother: "We have had some correspondence about my son [3633] and your Father's reading for him in which he foretold much that has come to pass. [3633] is now in...State Hospital. The doctors have of course, there and elsewhere in other sanitariums where he has been, labeled his trouble, dementia praecox, schizophrenia, etc.... Thank God his intellect seems intact, he writes for books he has always liked and he takes two newspapers..."

Report from file: [3633] died on 12/31/63. 3633-1 Reports

Just as is evidenced in the above case, the readings frequently stated that an individual's free will had an enormous impact upon his or her future. For that reason, precognition was much more subject to alteration and change, while clairvoyance, telepathy, and retrocognition were not. When Edgar Cayce predicted a future—for an individual, a nation, or even the world—it was a future based upon current events and probable directions. If events continued to move along the same course—if people's attitudes, activities, and external conditions remained the same—then Edgar Cayce could somewhere project this information onto a future time line and "see" the results. In spite of the many variables affecting precognition, time and again, what the readings saw came to pass.

In 1935, in an amazing display of precognitive perception, Edgar Cayce warned a twenty-nine-year-old freight agent of catastrophic events that were building within the international community. In response to a question regarding global affairs, the readings described an entire world at war. Although not seeing the picture as necessarily an unchangeable destiny, Cayce warned that "tendencies in the hearts and souls of men are such" that these conditions could be brought about:

As to the affairs of an international nature, these we find are in a condition of great anxiety on the part of many; not only as individuals but as to nations.

And the activities that have already begun have assumed such proportions that there is to be the attempt upon the part of groups to penalize, or to make for the associations of groups to carry on same.

This will make for the taking of sides, as it were, by various groups or countries or governments. This will be indicated by the Austrians, Germans, and later the Japanese joining in their influence; unseen, and gradually growing to those affairs where there must become, as it were, almost a direct opposition to that which has been the *theme* of the Nazis (the Aryan). For these will gradually make for a growing of animosities.

And unless there is interference from what may be called by many the *supernatural* forces and influences, that are activative in the affairs of nations and peoples, the whole *world*—as it were—will be set on fire by the militaristic groups and those that are "for" power and expansion in such associations. 416-7

An investment banker came to Edgar Cayce with a request for personal guidance as well as any information that might be provided of a "national and international" nature. The date was March 26, 1935, and the individual, Mr. [261], was interested in obtaining counsel regarding the financial stability of investments and the federal government. He was warned to wait until after April 15 to make any new investments because of some "unexpected activity" that might cause changes on the national scene. Cayce advised the gentleman that if the changes came, "then there *may* be anxiety in all directions for the American public" (261-14). When asked what kind of changes he was referring to, Cayce replied, "Accidents in officials of higher position." The reading continued:

> These associations, then, come from the sojourn of individuals in an environment such that the correlation of activities from many quarters will work with the individual's application of knowledge. Not that this is *destined* irrespective of what may happen! For many have been the calamitous conditions averted, even in this country— especially through the period of February. Again we are approaching same now, in between this and the 5th and 6th day of April, with the leader in this country—or Roosevelt, when there will be adverse conditions...261-14

Just as foretold in the information, ten days after the reading was given, there was an assassination attempt on the president's life. The AP news service released this story a week later:

> MAN WHO THREATENED ROOSEVELT FOUND INSANE.
> *Boston, April 12—(AP)*—Thomas F. Murphy, a 27-year-old unemployed laborer, who was arrested a week ago for threatening President Roosevelt with assassination, was reported tonight by U.S. Marshal John J. Murphy to have been found insane after observation at the Boston Psychopathic Hospital. 261-14 Reports

Rather than seeing events as fated or predestined, the Cayce readings described individuals as being instrumental in "co-creating" their lives. However, most frequently this process is overlooked in the rush and hassle of everyday life and in people not taking the time to become aware of events they are actually creating for their tomorrows. As one example, the readings suggested that individuals were forgetting their true spiritual nature. This neglect was setting events in motion that would create turmoils and strife within the country. In June 1939, while giving a reading on "the American nation, its ideals, principles and purposes," Edgar Cayce predicted the outcome:

> Ye are to have turmoils—ye are to have strifes between capital and labor. Ye are to have a division in thine own land before there is the second of the Presidents that next will not live through his office—a mob rule! 3976-24

Some contend that this reading may have foretold the death of Franklin Roosevelt, the assassination of John F. Kennedy, and the race riots of the 1960s. Again, rather than being preordained, in this same reading Cayce advised the nation to "give God a chance." By so doing, he said, individuals would begin to remember their spiritual nature and there would be no racial or social problems within the United States, the natural result of there being "more of patience, more tolerance, more thought of others..." (3976-24).

Rather than requesting information on the nation or the world as a whole, most frequently individuals were interested in events that affected them closer to home—in their personal lives and in their communities. The Cayce files are filled with predictions of this nature. For example, in July 1932, a land developer from the Norfolk/Virginia Beach area was interested in the potential growth of the city and its surroundings. Here is a portion of the reading, along with case file reports:

> With the years that are to come, conditions that are to arise, as we find, eventually—and this within the next thirty years—Norfolk, with its environs, is to be the chief port on the East coast, this not excepting Philadelphia or New York; the second being rather in the New England area...
>
> (Q) What is the future of Virginia Beach?
> (A) This, as we find, would require a great deal of speculation on the part of individuals. As we would find, and as we would give, of all the resorts that are in the East coast, Virginia Beach will be the first and the longest lasting of the increasing of the population, valuation, and activities. Hence, as we would give, the future is *good*...5541-2
>
> The *Virginian-Pilot,* Sunday, 3/15/70: BEACH GOES BOOM ... The history of Virginia Beach as a town actually began...[with] the construction of a clubhouse for

hunting and fishing in 1880...A few summer cottages were built along the oceanfront and the occupants traveled by the railroad from Norfolk...By the end of 1962, there were 8,718 residents in the tiny area incorporated as Virginia Beach, and 91,307 people in adjoining Princess Anne County. The two merged on Jan. 1, 1963...The city has experienced a tremendous population boom...and the total figure is now almost 180,000. The 50-mile-long city is known as the "world's largest resort city"...[By 1979, the city was home to 250,000 residents, and by 2006, Virginia Beach had become the most populated city in the state with approximately 450,000 residents.]

Report from the *Virginian-Pilot*, Wednesday, 9/3/80: PORT'S TONNAGE MAY PASS N.Y.'s. Norfolk—The Virginia Port Authority predicted Tuesday that in 1980, for the first time, the tonnage of goods shipped through Hampton Roads may equal or surpass the total shipped by New York City–New Jersey, the East Coast's largest port...5541-2 Reports

Children and young people often received life readings, outlining career possibilities for their lives. In 1939, a nineteen-year-old college student, interested in his future and the line of work for which he would be best suited, obtained this reading:

In the present, then, as indicated, the entity has the ability...to become a judge or a chooser of those influences for conservation—that *must* become more and more a part of man's experience, especially in the environ in which this entity has come.

Hence, as indicated, the entity has a definite mission—not only in making for the material gains for its own land and peoples and nations, but to spiritualize those purposes also, rather than the conservation of power or might without a channel or outlet for the emotions of the spiritual nature of man himself...

As to the abilities of the entity in the present, then, and that to which it may attain, and how:

As to the choice of how the entity will act itself, as to what is to be the choice of its ideals—that is alone to the entity.

For the urges and impulses may be magnified or minimized by the very power of the mind and impulse within itself.

As to whether it is to be for the fulfilling of that for which it entered, or for the glorifying of self or a cause or a purpose, or an individual, must be chosen by the entity.

In those fields of conservation, not only that is with government, with the activity of nations—whether it be of fishes in waters, birds of certain calibre or needs for food, or for the varied manners that they give protection to certain portions of the land, or timbers or the better conservation of soil for certain seeds or crops—all of these are the channels as we find in which the entity may find contentment and harmony, and the better outlet for fulfilling that purpose for which the entity entered this experience.

Ready for questions...

(Q) How should I expend my energies...?
(A) Just as indicated.

There have been and are in those fields especially the attempt of the Government to lay out plans whereby man may be taken from various portions of the land or environ where there is less opportunity; but here there is the taking of the activity of the raw and converting it into man's use! But man must learn—as the entity may particularly aid in—to conserve these very natures in whatever portion of the land he already resides!

Of course, the land continues to grow—for it is God's footstool. Man's abuse of same gives way to those things such that it becomes no longer productive. But if there is the conservation of its strength—the lands, the timbers, and God's creatures that manifest through same—it is a continuous thing. For "Ye grow in grace and in knowledge and in understanding" is applicable to man's secular life just as much as to his mental or spiritual...1931-1

More than thirty years later, a report was filed in the form of a questionnaire completed and returned by Mr. [1931] in February 1972:

1. What jobs have you held since your reading? (In chronological order)
   Timber Cruiser, U.S. Forest Service
   Ranger-Naturalist, U.S, National Park Service
   U.S. Park Ranger, U.S. National Park Service
   U.S. Game Management Agent, U.S. Fish and Wildlife Service

2. Have you ever spoken with Edgar Cayce? (Yes) (No)
   Yes.
   How well, if so, did you know him?
   Corresponded frequently while working for the U.S. Forest Service in Alaska as well as spoke to him at the June conferences at Virginia Beach and after life reading and check readings.

3. Do you feel that Edgar Cayce's source of information depicted you accurately?
   No doubt about it.

4. At the time of the reading, did you have confidence in his counseling? (Yes) (No)
   Yes.

5. Do you feel that the reading helped you? How?
   By giving direction to natural urges. After following the advice in the readings I have been truly happy in

my life's work. With Edgar Cayce's "road map" the journey has been great in the conservation field.

6. As you look back, do you see patterns that were shown in the readings that you didn't see before? Please explain.
   No. I think everything mentioned in the readings was accurate in my case from the start. It was only a matter of getting on with life's work. At the time of the reading I knew the information was correct and nothing has changed my mind. 1931-1 Reports

In a number of readings, personal counsel branched out into information that affected many more individuals than simply the questioner. For example, a forty-three-year-old realtor interested in commodity futures asked, in August 1926, for a year-end weather forecast:

As for the weather conditions, and the effect same will produce on various portions of the earth's sphere, and this in its relation to the conditions in man's affairs: As has been oft given, Jupiter and Uranus influences in the affairs of the world appear the strongest on or about October 15th to 20th—when there may be expected in the minds, the actions—not only of individuals but in various quarters of the globe, destructive conditions as well as building. In the affairs of man many conditions will arise that will be very, very, strange to the world at present—in religion, in politics, in the moral conditions, and in the attempt to curb or to change such, see? For there will be set in motion [that indicating] when prohibition will be lost in America, see? Violent wind storms—two earthquakes, one occurring in California, another in Japan—tidal waves following, one to the southern portion of the isles near Japan. 195-32

Report compiled by a geologist for the 195-32 case file: "The following excerpts are from the *Monthly Weather Review* for October 1926 (U.S. Weather Bureau, 1926): 'October was an exceptionally stormy month and the number of days with gales was considerably above the normal over the greater part of the [North Atlantic] ocean. Several tropical disturbances occurred during the month, three of which were of slight intensity, but the storm that created such havoc in Cuba on the 20th was one of the most severe on record' (p. 435). In the vicinity of the Kuril Islands, 'the westerly winds increased to hurricane force on the 14th and 15th...' Reports from ships in the vicinity of the Philippines Islands 'indicate 3 and probably 4 violent storms [typhoons] during the early part of October 1926 (p. 438). Reports of storms in the southern hemisphere for 1926 are difficult to obtain or lacking entirely. The closest one may come in most cases are the reports in the *India Weather Review*.' This publication states (p. 110) that 'a moderate storm occurred the 15th to the 18th of October in Andaman Sea.'

"The California earthquake of October 22, 1926, was composed of three strong shocks... 'the principal shocks were perceptible over probably 100,000 square miles.' (U.S. Coast and Geodetic Survey, 1951, p. 26) The previous strong shock reported (ibid., p. 26) for California was on July 25, 1926, and the following strong shock was on January 1, 1927. Three earthquakes occurred in Japan on the 19th and 20th of October 1926 (Anon., 1926, pp. 340–342), but these were not relatively strong shocks and, apparently, there were no 'tidal waves following.' If 'southern portion of the isles near Japan' may be taken to mean the Solomon Islands, however, then consideration should be given to the shock of September 18, 1926, that produced a sea or 'tidal' wave which 'inundated the whole island of Kokomaruki and part of Guadalcanal' (Heck, 1947, p. 283)." 195-32 Reports

During the course of a physical reading given for one individual, the reading foresaw future medical advancements that might make diagnosis from a drop of blood a possibility. The reading was given in 1927—at a time when the prediction would have been considered the makings of science fiction:

For, as is seen, there is no condition existent in a body that the reflection of same may not be traced in the blood supply, for not only does the blood stream carry the rebuilding forces to the body, it also takes the used forces and eliminates same through their proper channels in the various portions of the system. Hence we find red blood, white blood and lymph all carried in the veins. These are only separated by the very small portions that act as builders, strainers, destroyers, or resuscitating portions of the system—see? Hence there is ever seen in the blood stream the reflections or evidences of that condition being carried on in the physical body. The day may yet arrive when one may take a drop of blood and diagnose the condition of any physical body...283-2

Twenty years later, Dr. Laurence H. Snyder of Ohio University, speaking at the New York Academy of Medicine, told a large audience: "It would be possible for me to take a drop of blood from each of you in the audience tonight; then five years later I could return here, gather you together and take another drop of blood. Without knowing the source of the bloods, I could then assign the correct sample to the proper person."

This was a striking statement at that medical meeting; it gave some idea of the enormous gain in knowledge about human blood. It was also brought out that more facts had been gathered in the forty-eight months prior to that meeting than were collected in the previous forty-eight years. Yet Edgar Cayce, twenty years before, had predicted such a development. 254-3 Reports

12/27/69 Clipping from *Dallas News*: PINPRICK OF BLOOD TELLS ALL. *New York (WMNS)*—A single pinprick of blood can now yield as much medical information as an entire syringe full. At the moment, new "microchemical techniques" are used only for babies, whose blood supply is limited and precious, and only in certain pediatric centers. But Dr. Knud Engel of Babies Hospital, who helped develop the microchemical technique in Denmark, says the technique may become routine for babies and may spread to adults within five years.

The conventional method of obtaining a blood sample involves tapping a vein in the elbow crease for a syringeful. Arteries must be punctured for special tests. Using the microchemical technique, a foot or a hand is warmed, which increases the arterial blood flow. When sophisticated, miniaturized electronic equipment is used to analyze a pinprick of this blood, the results are as valid as for a large quantity of arterial blood, Dr. Engel says. 283-2 Reports

The following selection of case histories also demonstrate the wide variety of precognitive information provided by the Edgar Cayce readings.

IN AN EARLY reading given in 1919, a pregnant woman was treated by a doctor for a disease she did not have. The treatment led to complications and, eventually, two operations performed by another surgeon. Despite the operations, the woman's health continued to decline. Three additional doctors were called in; all stated that the woman could not possibly live much longer and would die before giving birth, killing both mother and child. As a last resort, Edgar Cayce was contacted by the family. In the reading, he confirmed that it was too late to save the mother but that she would live long enough to give birth to the child and that the child would survive. Cayce gave a prescription that immediately made the woman feel more comfortable. When the time finally came, a baby girl was born. The child was so small and frail that the doctors advised against wasting a name on the infant; she would surely die. However, their prognosis was incorrect. The mother lived ten days after giving birth, and the child grew to adulthood, eventually married, and had two daughters of her own (4925-1).

IN A CASE from 1923, a man was alarmed to find his vision seriously declining. Concerned for his sight, he contacted Edgar Cayce. In the reading, Cayce stated that nerves to the eyes were being strangled but that a complete healing could be achieved in just nineteen days. The procedure recommended by the readings was to be performed as soon as possible before serious and permanent damage occurred. Cayce advised surgery that was unheard of by the family's doctors.

The reading gave instructions as to how the operation for the eyes was to occur through the individual's nostril! The doctors warned against taking such drastic measures, and the recommendations were not followed. Less than two years later, the man was almost completely blind (3740-1).

In 1926, a thirty-eight-year-old man was told that his present employer was dissatisfied with his performance, but not to worry—he would receive at least three business opportunities in the near future. Within a few days, he received a letter from his present employer regarding his job performance, as well as the predicted three job offers (779-15).

A thirty-six-year-old man—wondering if he would ever get married—was told that in his "fortieth year you should find a happy union in marriage." When he was forty, he actually did get married, to a woman he had not even known at the time of the reading (3343-1).

In September 1933, a forty-year-old sales manager was told that "by the 7th of December there should be hard liquor in the United States." (257-121) On December 5, 1933, the Twenty-first Amendment, repealing Prohibition, was passed by a joint resolution of Congress.

ON JANUARY 24, 1935, in a brief side comment during a reading, Edgar Cayce predicted an illness for the king of England in the coming year (270-33). Although the Cayce family had no connection or contact with the king, it was later discovered that—despite medical advice to the contrary—King George V insisted on wintering in England. As a result, he succumbed to a chill and died on January 20, 1936.

FACED WITH THE possibility of bankruptcy, a sixty-nine-year-old man was concerned that his son's company would be sold at auction. The reading correctly predicted that the company would, instead, be taken over by another party (304-3).

FREQUENTLY, PREGNANT WOMEN asked Edgar Cayce when they could expect the birth of their children, and he told them. In a number of instances, at the parents' request, he named the sex, and in case 575-1 he told the date of birth, the sex, and the approximate weight of the infant.

A YOUNG WIDOW, seeking assistance in finding her proper line of work, was advised against riding, driving, or walking near railroad crossings for the next few months. A week later, the woman was driving her car down the street (near the train tracks) when, suddenly, a man drove through the railroad crossing and ran right into her car. Thankfully, neither the woman nor the driver of the other car was fatally injured (771-1).

IN 1942, WHEN SHIPS, trains, and automobiles were the major modes of transportation, an individual asked about the future of the airplane. Cayce replied, "This, to be sure— air transportation—will become more and more the basis of *all* relationships with other nations, countries, as well as the internal or national activity" (416-17).

PARENTS OF A two-day-old child were warned that their son could one day suffer an accident to his extremities. Nearly four years later, one month before the boy's fourth birthday, he fell down a back stairwell and cut an artery in his temple. Thankfully, the next-door neighbor, a doctor, arrived within seconds and quickly stitched the wound without anesthetic, for there wasn't enough time. Because of the doctor's quick action, the boy survived (3069-1).

AN EXTREMELY WEALTHY and prominent New York businessman obtained a reading for his health and was told that if he followed the readings' suggestions for treatment, diet, and exercise, he would have "many years of useful service and activity..." However, if he did not follow the recommendations, he was warned that he would not live much longer. Even though a doctor agreed with Cayce's findings and wanted to follow the treatment, the businessman thought otherwise. Three months later, the man died (1684-1).

A THIRTY-FOUR-YEAR-OLD New York investor was told that his greatest success would come in the field of travel, trade, or commerce—especially in tropical countries, specifically Brazil, Ceylon, India, or Persia. By 1962, the individual had become a U.S. ambassador to Iran, the former Persia (1416-1).

IN FEBRUARY 1925, during a life reading for a twenty-six-year-old physician, Cayce stated that the young doctor would soon find himself in possession of a great deal of money. The reading advised him to exercise caution and discretion in caring for his wealth, especially in the face of "adverse forces that will come then in 1929" (2723-1). Somehow, the sleeping Cayce may have seen the disastrous stock market crash more than four and a half years before its occurrence!

IN AN EFFORT to demonstrate the extensive documentation maintained by the Edgar Cayce Foundation, two additional case histories are presented here in detail. The first is the case of Fredrica Fields, a young woman whose talent with stained glass was accurately predicted in her reading. The second is that of Colonel Edmund Starling—a White House Secret Service agent who wished to write a book about his personal experiences with five U.S. presidents.

Fredrica H. Fields (499-2)—Because of her parents' fascination with the work of Edgar Cayce, a young woman named Fredrica Fields requested a reading in 1934. Not showing much interest in the material herself, she set the reading aside. Years later, she told a newspaper reporter, "At the time he did it, it meant nothing to me. It went in one ear and out the other." Time passed, and Fredrica became a housewife and a mother, forgetting all about the information that had been given to her by Edgar Cayce. In fact, it was not until her mother died that Fredrica found the reading among some of her mother's personal papers. In 1977, Fredrica contacted the Edgar Cayce Foundation to inform the staff of the accuracy of what her reading had foretold. In part, her reading stated:

> The influences from Mercury show the high mental abilities; with the Aquarian influence in its relationships to the Jupiterian making for abilities in certain given lines of activity. And these, as we find, will change, do change, as developments are applied in the experience of the entity in its relation to the active influences in the present sojourn. For, as in the present, certain types of art and its relation-

ships to activities in individuals' lives may make for an influence in the present activities. And there will come those periods when the activities in relation to art, that has to do with a great deal more of that as from stained glass or those that make for activities in the prism reactions to influences as related to things and to people, will be of a greater interest; as also music of a certain character or nature, or nature studies will become the more active in the experience of the entity as changes come...

Hence, the abilities in the present and that to which it may attain, and how, may be added also in these:

One having an analytical mind. One that may mete for individual activity much that may be helpful; for much may be given by the entity in its associations and relations among individuals.

And in those fields that are innately and manifestedly in the experience in the present, of the art, of the music, and especially that which may come in those that may make for the light through such activities to others, the entity may gain the knowledge of self—and in gaining the knowledge of self make applicable in the experience its relationships to others, thus bringing the greater development in this experience...

May the entity then in its own development find, and know through those things that have been given here, that in the study and in the application of same in the present experience may the entity come to know self better and in whom and in what it may believe.

Seek; for only the seeker may find. Do .not lose confidence in self. Know in what thou hast believed, and if it does not answer to that thou hast set as thine ideal—know it will turn to but clay, and thus only reach the satisfying of cravings. But let thine heart, thine mind, thine soul, be joyous in that thou hast gained in thine experience, that to express love in thine activities to thy neighbor is the greater service that a soul may give in this mundane sphere. 499-2

March 1977: "Imagine my surprise to find the following in my life reading: 'and there will come those periods when the activities in relation to art, that has to do with a great deal more of that as from stained glass'...I was deep in the study of stained glass, with a deep inner feeling that this was to be my life. Mr. Cayce went on to say music and nature would also be important to me. These three things—next to my family—are my life. I am enclosing a few papers for you in the hope they may be of interest because of the prophecy of what I would do. I thought there might be someone studying this aspect of the readings...

"It might also be of interest to you that I am self taught in the field of stained glass, and have developed this original approach on my own that is quite different from anyone else's work, either in the U.S. or Europe. A number of books and magazines have given space to my techniques..." 499-2 Reports

Fredrica Fields also reported that she had been a student of voice and ballet and that she could play the piano and the organ. In fact, she stated, she "could not live without music." She also tended a large garden in order to raise her own organic fruits and vegetables. She had won awards at the Corcoran Gallery of Art and the National Collection of Fine Arts at the Smithsonian Institution for her stained-glass work. Because the reading so accurately depicted the kind of person she would become, in August 1977, Fredrica and her husband, Brigadier General Kenneth E. Fields, visited the A.R.E. to take measurements for two sets of stained-glass windows she wished to donate to the organization. When completed, each window consisted of three panels, measured twenty feet in length and weighing three hundred pounds. A headline from the December 7, 1978, issue of a Virginia Beach paper, *The Beacon,* said: ARTIST FULFILLS CAYCE PREDICTION.

In 1992 Fredrica died at the age of eighty. Her obituary is the final report in her case file:

Fredrica H. Fields, 80, a nationally known and widely exhibited stained glass artist, died of natural causes March 4 at Greenwich Hospital. A resident of Greenwich for 33 years, she was creating stained-glass windows up to the time of her death. Her most recent installations were two windows at The Church of the Holy Comforter in Kenilworth, Ill. Regarded as a pioneer and innovator in the field of abstract stained-glass windows, Mrs. Fields received inquiries and requests for her windows from as far away as Saudi Arabia and India. While stained-glass windows are usually associated with cathedral windows depicting biblical scenes, hers are abstract designs using layers of different types of glass of varied shapes and colors. Mrs. Fields had taught classes at the Greenwich YWCA and her work was shown in exhibits of The Greenwich Art Society and the Stamford Art Association. She was a member of the Stained-Glass Association of America, from which she received several first-place commendations. Locations of her glass installations include the Greenwich YWCA, the Cole Auditorium of the Greenwich Library, St. John's Episcopal Church in Stamford, The National Cathedral in Washington, D.C., The Connecticut Hospice in Branford, Concordia College in Bronxville, N.Y., and the Association for Research and Enlightenment Meditation Center in Virginia Beach, Va. Additionally, her works are part of the permanent collection of glass at the Corning Museum in Corning, N.Y.

Colonel Edmund Starling (3182-1)—Colonel Edmund W. "Bill" Starling was a Secret Service agent in the White House for nearly thirty years. During his career, he personally served five presidents (Wilson, Harding, Coolidge, Hoover, and Roosevelt). At sixty-seven, it was his desire to retire and to write a book that would detail his White House experiences. Seeking advice, he spoke to a personal friend, David Kahn, and asked for suggestions regarding his book project. For years, Kahn had been a supporter and enthusiast of the Edgar Cayce readings. It was Kahn who recommended that the colonel obtain a reading.

In August 1943, before the reading had even been given, Thomas Sugrue, Cayce's biographer and also a friend of Kahn's, expressed interest in the book project. His enthusiasm comes through in the following letter, contained in Colonel Starling's case file:

Letter from Thomas Sugrue to David E. Kahn: "This is the tale of one man's observation of the most important events in the history of man. When Starling went to the White House for his first assignment...the civilized world was largely lighted by kerosene and gas. Telephones were uncommon. Movies were, like airplanes, in the experimental stage. Radio was unknown. Democracies were the exception to the rule in government...etc.... we give a picture of the world about to make the big change...

"Often it has been said—'If the walls could talk.' Now here is a wall or chair, or desk, as it were, which saw all of history unroll through the presidents of the U.S. from Roosevelt I to Roosevelt II. This wall now talks. Here is the story, the intimate story, of these men—how they came to office buoyant, strong, hopeful, full of faith and determination—how they encountered disappointment, tragedy, disillusion—how they went from office broken, ready to die—how the world rolled over them, a giant steam-roller which they tried with their pitiful efforts to steer away from the common people.

"It is the story of man's fight against his own inclination to take the easy way—it is the record of man's will, determination, prodigality, immorality, irresponsibility, and final achievement—told through its reflection in the personification of the American man's character and thought—the White House." 3182-1 Reports

When the reading took place, five people were present in the room: Edgar Cayce, Gertrude Cayce, Gladys Davis, Colonel Starling, and David Kahn:

(Q) Reference the publication of a book on my life, activities and experience—please give the plan which will tell a fascinating story, of value and interest to the nation as a whole.
(A) This would present a phase of human experience, a phase of human relationships that would be unique; not only fascinating but could, if properly written and presented, prove a helpful influence in the present emergencies; setting an example, an ideal, for many a young man, that would make such a life story most helpful to this day and age. For, it represents a unique experience in the history of the nation, and may be presented from an angle

that will not only prove beneficial to post war experiences again but will clarify for many some of those experiences that have been in fear or doubt by some through many periods of development...

Do not present *any* political factions. For, as the entity in its abilities and in its activities acted—and is acting—in the capacity for the love of God and of country—and the man directing the affairs of a nation perchance using the opportunity—as observed by a servant of the people—to the glory of God. *That* is the manner of presentation of this entity's service to a nation...

(Q) Who would be the best publisher to do the job?
(A) As we find, a serial in such as Collier's; published by such as Simon & Schuster... 3182-1

The reading then confirmed that Thomas Sugrue would be capable of working with Colonel Starling on the project and stated, "...you will not find a better individual." A final suggestion was offered:

...To be sure, there might be those who would seek to inject—some publishers would ask for—sensation. That is not the order of the day. Throughout the whole experience of each administration from the beginning with Roosevelt to the end in another Roosevelt, there are human interest incidents. The greater human interest stories should be about that administration least understood. Clarify some in others; not as political issues or as of telling or indicating even State secrets of *any* nature. Then present the *great opportunity* of the American nation, and missing the boat—in the Peace Conference. These are the great themes, and those that—when the entity searches his own self— find the greater appeal to the inner man. 3182-1

In other readings, Cayce had repeatedly stated that the United States had been remiss in not accepting Woodrow Wilson's plan for a League of Nations. After this gentle rebuff, additional advice was given, including the reminder that "no politics" were to be a part of the book. Colonel Starling then asked a final question:

(Q) How much should be said of present day visitors at White House known to me?
(A) Enough to indicate the needs of the warnings. This is to the fellow man! not to laud any particular President, but principles—principles! Not to belittle any, as it will not be the purpose of the individual entity here presenting same; nor should it be sarcastic nor anything bordering upon same—by the one writing the story. The truth, sure—but *principle* first! And it will be, then, not merely a Best Seller but—for many years—the ideal of many an American. 3182-1

Armed with the information that Sugrue was the proper writer, that Simon & Schuster should be approached about publication, and that the book would be "not merely a Best Seller but...the ideal of many an American," Colonel Starling returned to Washington, and David Kahn headed home for New York. In an interview given in 1959 to *NBC's Monitor National Radio Show*, David Kahn described the next chain of events:

David Kahn:...I came onto New York and caught the only taxicab in Pennsylvania Station that was standing there at one o'clock in the morning...I looked over and saw a man in the back of the crowd with a big suitcase on his shoulder. I said, "You over there, with the big suitcase. Are you going up town?" I was embarrassed...all these people—one person, two people in a cab.

"Sure," he said. "I'm going up town and I'd like to ride."

I said, "Come on over."

He gets in, puts down his coat, puts down his suitcase. He says, "Schuster's my name."

I said, "You wouldn't be of Simon and Schuster?"

He says, "I'm Maxwell Schuster."

I said, "I'm David E. Kahn, and you're going to publish a book for me."

He says, "What book?"

I said, "*Starling of the White House...*"

David Kahn proceeded to tell Schuster about the reading with Edgar Cayce. Later, a lunch meeting was arranged among Schuster, Kahn, and Starling. Thomas Sugrue was hired to write the manuscript, and the book was eventually written. After publication, Maxwell Schuster occasionally referred to it as "the Cayce book" and, according to Kahn, gave an interview detailing the story of the ride in the cab, the reading given by Cayce, and the success of the publication.

In September 1943 the *Norfolk Ledger-Dispatch* featured an article, PRESIDENTIAL PROTECTOR TO RETIRE:

Washington, Sept. 20.—(AP)—Col. Edmund W. (Big Bill) Starling, 67-year-old Secret Service veteran who helped guard five presidents, will turn in his shooting irons around November 1 and retire to a less exciting life of fishing and hunting in Florida...

Starling joined the Secret Service on November 14, 1914, during the first administration of Woodrow Wilson. He became supervising agent of the White House detail during the first term of Franklin D. Roosevelt, but turned over that title to a much younger man, Michael F. Reilly, about a year ago.

Starling has traveled more than a million miles as a Secret Service man—with and in advance of traveling presidents, investigating routes and arranging police protection for them.

While retiring from government service, he says he will hold himself in readiness in [the] event his services are needed for the American delegation to the next peace gathering.

Although most of his 30 years as a Secret Service man were passed as a White House agent, Starling and his staff of husky young marksmen never have had to tangle with an attempted assassination in public. That, perhaps, explains Secret Service efficiency. Most of its work is preventive. 3182-1 Reports

Just as Cayce predicted, the book was published by Simon & Schuster. Unfortunately, neither Edgar Cayce nor Colonel Starling lived to see its release. In March 1946, the *Norfolk Ledger-Dispatch* featured a *Christian Science Monitor* review of the book, *Starling of the White House,* under the heading HE GUARDED PRESIDENTS FOR 30 YEARS:

There is nothing else in the whole world quite like the White House detail of the Secret Service. These men are primarily guardians of presidents, and they have successfully prevented catastrophe for nearly half a century. But more than guardians: they are comrades to presidents, they are diplomats, they are friends and confidants and they have helped to lighten the weary, lonely load of many a chief executive.

Chief among these remarkable men, indeed, unique among them, was Col. Edmund W. Starling. I have never met a more engaging, amiable, and utterly competent man. The first time I entered the White House, as a young reporter, I met him and immediately felt warmed by his welcome. And I was only one among many thousands in all parts of the United States who felt just the same way.

But I did not need friends, and sometimes presidents did, Colonel Starling was one of Calvin Coolidge's closest friends and companions. He taught the shy and stiff Vermonter to fish and humanized him perhaps more than anybody else ever did. He was deeply attached to Woodrow Wilson, although he spent many a cold night waiting on the sidewalk while President Wilson paid court to his second wife, Edith Bolling Galt. He felt a sympathy and pity for Warren Harding, and from direct observation he cleans up some lingering stains on President Harding's memory. Colonel Starling was not able to bring friendship to another lonely man: Herbert Hoover. And Franklin Roosevelt had many friends already, although he and Colonel Starling were very close.

All this rich and important tapestry of memories is delightfully recorded in *Starling of the White House*, a book put together in Colonel Starling's own words by Thomas Sugrue (New York: Simon & Schuster, $3). It tells more of two presidents at least, Wilson and Coolidge, than most of their biographies. It is a priceless aid to the historian…

The best stories are of Coolidge and Wilson. There is President Wilson walking down Connecticut Avenue dancing little jigs, after a courtship visit to Mrs. Galt, whistling: "Oh, you beautiful doll! You great big beautiful doll!" There is President Coolidge, asking Colonel Starling to lend him "ten." "Ten dollars?" asked Starling. "No, ten cents," said the president.

Always, Colonel Starling's deep religious sense is apparent. And his great gentleness, as well as his extreme competence in his job. His sharp eyes saw everything that might endanger his presidents. Yet best of all was not his negative job of protection, but his positive job of helping to enlighten and brighten the lives of these solitary leaders. 3182-1 Reports

By June 1946, *Starling of the White House* had sold more than 100,000 copies. Later, it became a Book-of-the-Month Club selection, and before it went out of print, it sold more than 200,000 copies.

EDGAR CAYCE'S PREDICTIONS ABOUT THE FUTURE OF THE PLANET

Over the years, perhaps the most frequently discussed and misquoted information regarding possible predictions of the future deals with Edgar Cayce's discussion of "earth changes." Although fewer than twenty of this type of reading exist, somehow this information has become some of the most prominent material contained in the Cayce files. Unfortunately, a number of books and articles have even taken this information out of context, setting aside the fact that humanity's co-creative involvement in building toward our collective future is rarely mentioned.

In truth, inevitable Earth changes are not discussed by the readings. Instead, Cayce saw the period between 1958 and 1998 as one of great change and transition. Apparently, during this forty-year period Cayce felt that the world would move toward becoming a global community rather than simply a conglomeration of fractured countries and rival powers. Eventually the emergence of a global community would result in an age of hope for all of humankind. Cayce saw this ultimate future as an "age of purity" in which individuals would see their responsibility toward one another, and all of humankind would have the ability to experience direct communication with the Divine (1602-3).

From Cayce's perspective, however, before a Golden Age becomes manifest, humankind has to undergo a number of challenges. In 1932, when asked to describe the principal events for the next fifty years affecting the welfare of the human race, Cayce had this to say:

> This had best be cast after the great catastrophe that's coming to the world in '36 (thirty-six), in the form of the breaking up of many powers that now exist as factors in the world affairs. 3976-10

Historically, although no major physical earthquakes resulted (neither did a predicted pole shift), 1936 did mark the outbreak of civil war in Spain, a declaration of war between China and Japan, and Hitler's reoccupation of the Rhineland—events which many pinpoint as the impetus for the eventual outbreak of World War II. Since the year did result in many changes as suggested by the readings, rather than earthquakes, the changes expressed themselves in the affairs of humankind through the outbreak of war.

In terms of Earth changes, some of the most disturbing readings were given between 1932 and 1934 and were directed at the period leading up to 1938. Often, these are the very readings that have been quoted out of context or have proven to be inaccurate. One example is the frequently quoted statement "The earth will be broken up in many places. The early portion will see a change in the physical aspect of the west coast of America…" (3975-15). What is misleading about quoting this reading is the fact that Cayce was actually responding to changes that might be expected to occur in *1934*!

Another basis for predictions regarding inundations for the western portion of the United States has been a dream Edgar Cayce once had about being born in the year A.D. 2158 on the coastline in the state of Nebraska. However, in a reading interpreting the dream, Cayce twice states that the foremost interpretation was assurance that his work will survive in spite of his personal difficulties at the time, for he had just been arrested for practicing medicine without a license. The dream was not necessarily a prediction of his rebirth; nor was it about coming Earth changes; instead, it was a personal encouragement for him to continue his work in spite of the challenges he was then experiencing (294-185).

Although the source of the reading's information was most frequently Edgar Cayce's own higher self, on rare occasions other "entities" identified themselves during the course of the reading. And in several such instances, the source was proven incorrect. For example, one reading briefly mentioned physical earth changes that would occur in Norfolk, Virginia, "nearer to '58." At the end of the reading, the question was asked, "Who is giving this information?" and the response came, "Zorain. Student with Zoroaster..." 311-10. In one of the most foreboding readings on global cataclysmic change, the source identified itself by saying, "I, Halaliel, have spoken" 3976-15.

To be true to some individuals' interpretations of the material, however, there are readings that suggest the Earth could receive major physical changes and even a shifting of the poles. Undoubtedly, changes of this magnitude would have catastrophic effects upon all of humankind. Since these readings are fairly specific, should we expect the worst and anticipate their accuracy? Not necessarily.

One challenge that arises when working with psychic predictions is that they are completely subject to the activities and the free will of those individuals about whom the prophecy is foretold. In fact, reading 3976-23 explores global conditions during the Depression and the buildup to war and makes it clear that we are all individually responsible for what happens in the world around us. This means that a psychic can make predictions based only upon current events and thought-forms. These thoughts and events are then projected onto a future time-line, however, because of the very nature of predictions, they are not set in stone—nor are they unavoidable. When enough individuals combine, utilizing their free will in a positive direction, the potential future is altered.

An excellent example of this is the Old Testament story of Jonah. The prophet Jonah foresaw the destruction of Nineveh because of the people's own negative thoughts and deeds. God was not destroying the city; rather, the people were bringing about a destruction based upon their own selfishness and acts of hate toward one another. In order to help the people, Jonah predicted the city's downfall. As a result, the people banded together, changed their thoughts and actions, and through the use of unified free will altered their foreseen future *in less than forty days*! The destruction never came, and Nineveh was saved. Essentially the people transformed themselves and, in turn, transformed the city, rather than having external events in the city force them to undergo personal change.

One of the most interesting dynamics of people working together is that they can raise the vibration of energy and thought to a higher level. Simply stated, this means that actual physical Earth changes seen decades ago by Edgar Cayce could now be changes occurring on a different level.

Certainly, some earthquakes will continue as part of the natural physical evolution of the planet. But potentially even more influential changes could come from worldwide political turmoil, economic upheavals, religious wars, ecological disasters, climatic changes, and personal challenges not necessarily geological in nature. In fact, on one occasion Cayce suggested that the exact nature of what's coming is yet to be shaped. "As to the changes that are coming...these will, as indicated, depend upon what individuals and groups do about what they know respecting His will, His purpose with man" (1602-6).

In addition to an inevitable Golden Age for all of humankind, just what kinds of predictions did Edgar Cayce make about our collective future?

Edgar Cayce predicted that we would discover evidence of Atlantis and an Atlantean civilization that had once rivaled our own technologically. Cayce stated that evidence for this lost continent had been saved in three locations on Earth, each in a subterranean hall of records. These locations were given as Egypt, the Yucatán, and the remnants of what is now Bimini. When asked what the hall of records contained, the readings replied:

A record of Atlantis from the beginnings of those periods when the Spirit took form or began the encasements in that land, and the developments of the peoples throughout their sojourn, with the record of the first destruction and the changes that took place in the land, with the record of the sojournings of the peoples to the varied activities in other lands, and a record of the meetings of all the nations or lands for the activities in the destructions that became necessary with the final destruction of Atlantis and the buildings of the pyramid of initiation, with who, what, where, would come the opening of the records that are as copies from the sunken Atlantis; for with the change it must rise (the temple) again. 378-16

While the rest of the world was seeing China as an impoverished Third World country, Cayce predicted that China would have an enormous impact upon the global stage. On one occasion, Cayce told a group of people that eventually China would become "the cradle of Christianity, as applied in the lives of men," suggesting that the personal application of spiritual principles would become paramount to the Chinese people. Cayce then went on to caution that it would take a long time to manifest but that it was the country's destiny: "Yea, it is far off as man counts time, but only a day in the heart of God—for tomorrow China will awake" 3976-29.

On another occasion, when a thirty-six-year-old book publisher asked about China's destiny in 1943, just prior to his own trip to the country to serve in the capacity of a missionary, Cayce promised amazing changes in the country that would lead to more democracy and greater religious freedom. He also suggested that eventually the height of civilization would move from the West to the Chinese people: "And these will progress. For, civilization moves west" 2834-3.

The Cayce readings also had a great deal to say about the missing years of Jesus and they spoke of a "Second Coming," in which Jesus would return and once again try to fulfill the real purpose of His life and ministry—not religious conversion but personal application of spiritual principles on the Earth.

Cayce predicted that lifespan would greatly increase, that we would discover how to create a perpetual-motion machine, that there would eventually be a growth in consciousness and a renewed sense of spirituality all over the planet, and he believed that insights provided by his own readings would "change the thought of mankind in general in many directions" (254-37). When he was asked in 1944 which religious thought would lead the world toward the greatest amount of spiritual light and understanding, his reply was simply that "Thou shalt love the Lord thy God with all thine heart, and thy neighbor as thyself!" (3976-8). Perhaps, more than anything else, this is the ultimate promise of Cayce predictions for our collective future.

Not being limited to perceiving the future, Edgar Cayce seemed just as capable of peering with uncanny accuracy into our personal and global past.

CHAPTER 5

EXAMPLES OF RETROCOGNITION

While he was in the trance state, Edgar Cayce's ESP seemed equally adept at obtaining information from the present, the future, or the past. His ability to peer into the past with uncanny psychic accuracy was demonstrated repeatedly. Thousands of readings attest to the variety of material available in this manner: previous events in a questioner's life, including accidents or forgotten traumas; ancient history, including the geological evolution of the planet and details of tribes and civilizations that predate recorded history; even the previous lives of an individual. Sometimes, straightforward historical information regarding the present-life history of a person could also be confirmed immediately. In the case of a fifty-seven-year-old man, Edgar Cayce began the reading with a curious statement: "Nabisco—yes..." (4066-1) It was later discovered that "Nabisco" had been the man's childhood nickname.

At the beginning of each reading that dealt with the past, Cayce would often appear to focus on specific incidents that occurred during the individual's present lifetime. One example comes from a reading given to a forty-four-year-old New York housewife in 1943:

> Gertrude Cayce: You will give the relations of this entity and the universe, and the universal forces; giving the conditions which are as personalities, latent and exhibited in the present life; also the former appearances in the earth plane, giving time, place and the name, and that in each life which built or retarded the development for the entity; giving the abilities of the present entity, that to which it may attain, and how. You will answer the questions, as I ask them:

> Edgar Cayce: (In going back over years from the present—"right pretty little girl—'10—had the measles—'13—'14—'16—first real love affair—"—etc.) . . . [The reading went on to describe her emotional traits, her feelings, her desires, her dissatisfaction with life, and her desire to be somewhere else, etc.] 3253-2

Verbal report on 9/24/53: "I do not recall the exact year I had measles, but I do remember having them. The reading was right about my first real love affair—at 16; it was right about my being emotional. I have a large circle of friends, although I make friends very slowly I always keep a friend once I have made a friendship. My biggest problem is being easily hurt. I'm trying hard to learn how to overcome this. It is so true about my being dissatisfied and the hurts that seem to come to me. I would always want to have a home, but feel such an urge to travel that I often feel such an unrest..." 3253-2 Reports

In the life readings—those readings dealing with the subject of past lives and soul purpose—Edgar Cayce went back over the years from the present experience, briefly mentioning the years back to the individual's birth. For example, in 1937, a life reading was given to a woman who was born in 1883:

Edgar Cayce: (In going back over the years from present— "1931—such a diffusion of interests!—'30, '29—'18—such anxieties! '17—'98—yes, a change again in surroundings—'88—'83—How happy they were [parents] to have the entity!")

We have the record here of that entity now known or called [1479]. 1479-1

Frequently, when providing medical information, Cayce pinpointed the cause of a present difficulty as an injury the individual had received in the past:

In the nerve system, in the cerebrospinal nerves, we find in the region of the 4th, 5th and 6th dorsal there has been at times back a lesion produced by subluxation of one of the dorsals themselves. The subluxation has in part been alleviated. While the strangulation to the sympathetic nerves of the secondary cardiac have not been relieved, this produces the choking as is produced in the bronchials and larynx, and the asthmatic condition as produced in lungs proper. This then becomes reflexly to the bronchials, throat and lungs. At such times we find the blood surcharged. As given, at such times we find the other organs of the system become involved before or after through their cycle of functioning, as is produced by the overtaxed condition in the system...85-1

Mr. [257]'s letter of 3/28/25: "...Mr. [...] received a reading from you for his mother [85] today which was truly very wonderful. It checks absolutely and he tells me that his mother had an accident five years ago in which the top of her spine was injured, just below the neck. Your giving out all this without having seen her and without having any knowledge of the case makes it very wonderful indeed..." 85-1 Reports

All manner of information, from the ancient to the recent past, seemed available to Cayce. For example, throughout the years he was giving readings, several people asked him for insights into and interpretations of their dreams. Not only could the readings respond to this type of inquiry, but there also were occasions when even the dreamer had forgotten information that had come from his or her own subconscious mind. Somehow, from his trance state, Cayce knew whether or not a person had overlooked a portion of the dream, and he would provide it:

(Q) Saturday morning, June 6 [1925], I dreamed I was on horseback and fell off. The same morning I dreamed of my father at home in New Orleans and awakened thinking of Cayce.

(A) In the one of the horse and rider, as the messenger that comes to each and every individual, and the falling off the rejection of the message in this manner. In the second we again find correlations of mental and the subconscious forces with the dearer ones coming in that mental relation, with the awakening thought of that having heard, with the wonder of the interpretation of the rider. All dream is not given here, for the vision of the roadway, with the obstructions as seen, and the cause of the horse to shy causing rider to fall gives that of the conditions through which the mental forces must pass to reach the greater forces in an understanding manner. This very, very good...136-4

The Cayce readings provide a wealth of insights into the ancient world. A twenty-six-year-old actress was told that, in a former life, she had made cave paintings in mounds located in the northwestern portion of New Mexico and that they continued to exist (2665-2). In a number of readings, including 261-5, Cayce spoke of an ancient Egyptian pyramid that had yet to be discovered. Additional readings on Egypt stated that a "sealed room" of records had been buried in the area of the Sphinx as an ancient time capsule of a long-ago civilization and would be found when the time was right (378-16). In addition to discussing hidden archaeological sites and uncovered records of forgotten civilizations, Edgar Cayce claimed that the history of humankind went back some ten million years! Although much of this material may be impossible to verify, contemporary research has uncovered evidence to confirm some of the information given in Cayce's trance state. As one example, a number of readings discussed the fact that the Nile had changed its course over eons and had once emptied into the Atlantic Ocean:

> The Nile entered into the Atlantic Ocean. What is now the Sahara was an inhabited land and very fertile. What is now the central portion of this country, or the Mississippi basin, was then all in the ocean; only the plateau was existent, or the regions that are now portions of Nevada, Utah and Arizona formed the greater part of what we know as the United States...364-13

> In the one before this we find again in this same land now called Egypt (this before the mountains rose in the south, and when the waters called the Nile then emptied into what is *now* the Atlantic Ocean)...276-2

In those periods when the first change had come in the position of the land...when the Nile (or Nole, then) emptied into what is now the Atlantic Ocean, on the Congo end of the country. What is now as the Sahara was a fertile land...5748-6

As if to confirm some of the above, an article published in *Science* (August 1986) reported that the imaging radar from the U.S. space shuttle had discovered previously unknown river valleys beneath the driest part of the Sahara. Through satellite imaging and on-site archaeological investigations, it appeared that the present-day Nile had changed its course, once flowing across the Sahara, through Africa, and into the Atlantic Ocean! Only time will tell how many more of the readings' historical claims will eventually be verified.

In a letter to a forty-one-year-old businessman who had shown an interest in Cayce's work, Cayce attempted to explain how he believed the mind worked. His words may provide insights into how his talent for retrocognition was even possible:

From Edgar Cayce's letter of 1/14/35: "In our physical bodies we find that there are nerve centers running from every portion to the central nervous system—the brain. It is this central nervous system with which we *physically* make material manifestations. But *mind* itself, or that portion of the soul mind with which we contemplate things, may work independently of the body. Just as, having been in a place we can imagine or visualize ourselves in that place again—without physically going to it. The mind goes, and with the memory it has can recall it to consciousness. It isn't the conscious mind that recalls. It's the conscious mind that made the record of the memory upon the soul mind. Do you see what I mean?" 531-4 Reports

In 1935, a woman sought genealogical information and "family records" regarding her father, who was deceased. Although she knew her father had immigrated to America around 1889, she knew very little else about his background. The reading stated that, according to customs records, he had entered the United States in 1890. The reading provided the name of the ship upon which he had arrived and the ports of arrival and departure, then described additional family records that existed in a small church in Vienna, placed for safekeeping nearly half a century earlier in a small box under the pulpit, within the altar (863-1).

In another instance, after being provided with the name and address of a person in New York who wanted a reading, Cayce began with the statement: "Yes, we have been in this building before..." (921-1). The location was unfamiliar to the conscious Cayce and his office staff. However, after thorough checking, it did appear as though his unconscious mind had "seen" the building before—twenty-eight years and thousands of readings earlier!

After 1923, when reincarnation became a topic of exploration, individuals often requested a life reading to discover innate talents and the occupations for which they might be best suited. For the same reason, parents requested life readings for their children and newborn infants, hoping to provide them with appropriate training and guidance. On other occasions, people sought counsel from the life readings to discover the roots of their unhappiness. The readings indicated that patterns established in past lives produced tendencies and probabilities in the present. Those patterns and tendencies must be faced—enabling the individual to become a better person in the process.

In reading 1541-11, a woman with an extreme aversion to the Catholic Church was told that her feelings resulted from events she had experienced nearly two thousand years earlier. Cayce stated that she had taken part in disagreements that arose between the followers of Peter and those of Paul. Those disagreements had led to her present anger and animosity toward the organized Church. It was time, however, to let go of the past. Her reading encouraged her to condemn no one and to learn instead to overcome this senseless antagonism. Apparently, she was given just that opportunity, as her daughter later reported:

Daughter's note: "My brother...married a Catholic... Mother was so distressed—said she would rather see her son dead than marry a Catholic. I do not recall many instances in Mother's life when she was more distressed. Later she became very close to [the brother's wife] in many ways, she had to admit that her good points were many, although she never has gotten over the deep feeling of prejudice toward the Catholic religion..." 1541-11 Reports

In 1929, a life reading was requested for a one-month-old baby boy. As with other life readings, Cayce detailed the child's past lives that had the greatest bearing upon the present and would be most helpful in explaining the boy's abilities to the parents. The reading began with the astrological influences that seemed to have an influence upon this soul, and then went on to describe the child's past lives and present-day tendencies and possibilities. Much of the reading is provided here in order to illustrate the typical format of a personal life reading:

Yes, we have the entity and those relations with the universe and universal forces, as are latent in the present experience. In the entering, astronomically we find the entity coming under the influence of Aries, the Moon, Venus, Jupiter, Mercury, with adverse influences in Neptune and benevolent influence in Arcturus and in the Uranian activities—especially as related to influences as come with Jupiter and Uranus when square with Venus, for we have an influence at the time that would be unusual as to Uranian, Jupiterian, and of Venus—for these are as *benevolent* influences for *this* entity. Being then out of the ordinary in the Uranian influence.

In the influences—these, as seen, may be given only as tendencies as may be builded in the present experience, and these may be altered or changed by the training or the environmental conditions, as well as the will of the entity. The *training*, then, may be in accord with the tendencies and thus bring harmony, peace, and an influence worth while, or the entity may be trained in opposition to tendencies and bring consternation and troubled conditions in the entity's experience in the present earth's plane, even to the extent where there may be physical forces affected in the individual—as has often been pointed out.

Tendencies, then, as we find with this entity...

Those of the tendencies toward that of strong, healthy, bright, and toward that of the art and of the influences *of* art in the life. This, then, covering a vast field—and may be brought into any of the channels as would be in keeping with that of the tendency, especially of delving into wood and its relations with those of arts and those of the precious stones, and as related to the influence *of* such in the lives of individuals as are makers, keepers, or as those that are bringing about such changes in the material forces and conditions of the universe in its whole to such conditions. Then, training and keeping in such lines will bring to the body those of conditions that will be the more satisfactory in the present experience.

Those of which the body are to be warned and kept from:

Those of water and of influence—any influence—that water or waterways bring in the elements of the material experiences for the entity; though there will be the natural tendency to investigate such by the entity, and these should be gradually discouraged rather than assisted towards such. Not discouraged in the manner as forbidden; for to forbid a thing to the entity is to make it determine to know the end of that thought as is sought concerning same. Rather, then, by reason and by explanation of elements that are detrimental to the best interests of the body, so train as to keep these in the background, but not forbidden.

In the abilities of the entity, these may be seen from those influences as has been in the experiences through which the entity has passed—for the entity would make a *great* physician. In the appearances, then—

In the one before this we find in that period when the preparations were being made for revolution in the present abode of the entity, when there was the suasion from withdrawal, or the establishing of a liberty loving people into that of a oneness in purpose of *own* rule. The entity in the name Ivan Dorr. The entity then in that position of ruling those that were disabled in a physical and material sense in the land now about which the body has again entered, and in the heights as are above the city there may be seen evidences of this entity's labors in the physical sense—on the mounds above the palisades. In the influence this has in the present experience, that tendency of the investigator as to intrinsic values and of intrinsic worth; yet not *always* measuring same by *material* worth. Get the variation! for this, as will be seen, will be an outstanding condition in the entity's development; that is, a busybody, an inquisitive body, but not one that may be termed a meddler into other peoples' affairs for the curiosity of the thing.

In the one before this we find in that period in the Roman rule when there were persecutions for the individuals who acclaimed the faith of the Nazarene. The entity then among those who were in power to administer the punishments meted out, and became a believer through the faith as shown by those so persecuted. Then in the name Eldoirn, and in the employ of the persecutor Nero. In this experience the entity gained through that of the ability to change the mind, and to act as the change would indicate in the physical and mental experiences of the body, *developing* high in this experience; and in the present there may be seen that of one determined and one set; one not loathful in activity or in mind, but one that should be trained rather to play as well as labor physically, for one in *this* development may become one-sided—without the proper guiding of a whole, full, oneness of purpose. In the influence as will be seen in the developing of the entity, one that will be set—yet will not be so set, unless improperly trained, as not to be able to be shown that one is ever in the state of development, or of growth, in mind as well as in body. One that may gain the inner knowledge of spiritual effects in the material plane and make physical application of same.

In the one before this we find in the rebuilding of the Holy City. The entity among those who ministered to the needs of the ailing and the sick, and was the physician in this period to Ezekiel—who led this return. In the name Zedkahi, and the entity gained and lost through this experience—gaining in the application of self to those who labored in the cause; losing in the selfish stand as taken against those who persecuted the builders—and brought to self condemnation for self in the attitude assumed. In the influence in the present experience, the tendency toward the desire to know as concerning physical ills—yet loath to give sufficient time to learn well. This, as seen, is as contradictory to some influences given. Hence that of the influence to guide in the moulding stage to where sincerity and purpose must be, one, and the full knowledge before the application can be that as a basis for full development . . . 759-1

In addition to providing counsel to the parents, the reading described the child's character traits and innate talents. Note that the information suggested he would make "a *great* physician" and later gave a past life in Jerusalem when he had been employed in that very occupation. At a later date, Cayce told the boy's parents that the child should not be forced into this direction, but instead should be encouraged if the boy did, in fact, show the intelligence and the inclination to become a doctor. With this in mind, subsequent reports prove extremely interesting:

From [759]'s mother when he was ten: "I met three little girls on the train coming in Saturday and they told me that my son was very naughty—that he had operated on a [dead] squirrel that he had found in the woods and brought in the liver, heart and kidneys to show the class. Now the teacher has decided to get him a set of doctor's implements so he can operate on another squirrel in front of the class..."

Report from 10/27/39: "[759] was elected president of 500 student body—the student council."

From father's letter on 11/4/40: "[759] made the honor roll and newspaper at High School."

Report when [759] was twelve:..."[He had] measles about two weeks ago. He looked it up and made the diagnosis himself, before the doctor came. He is definitely showing signs of physician tendencies..." 759-1 Reports

Later reports stated that [759] went to Harvard, interned at a large eastern hospital, specialized in psychiatry, and later became an outstanding physician in his field.

On another occasion, a forty-seven-year-old woman was told that she had been in and around Rome during the period when the Christians were persecuted. In a letter to Cayce received shortly after her reading was given, the woman wondered whether this might be the cause of her childhood fear:

Letter of 5/15/34: "You state that during my Roman life I was among the persecuted Christians. Here is a strange thing: often I've looked for the why of it and now I wonder if this is it. From my early childhood I've had a horrible fear of lions and tigers. When circus parades were in town and everyone turned out to see them, my favorite sister always took me by the hand to see them. I loved her and wanted to be with her, but though I liked everything else and always wanted to see the parades, the minute the cages of lions and tigers came I began to cry—to be panic-stricken and beg to be taken home. Poor unselfish girl, she wasn't bothered by them, but home she took me. Always the same performance—I had to go, but the fright was too much for me; no one knew why. Once I ran from the animal tent at Ringling's Circus, a girl in my teens, leaving friends, when a lion roared. And always at intervals I've had dreadful nightmares, and dreams of lions after me—I'd be holding a door with what strength I had against a lion. This bothered me so that I never would read or see pictures of them if I could avoid it, because of the reaction. My sister said when she knew you were going

to give me a reading, 'Maybe you had an experience earlier with lions.' When you wrote about the persecutions, I
wondered if perhaps this explains the fear within. What
do you think?" 541-1 Reports

Whenever he gave a reading, Edgar Cayce's primary goal
was to provide people with material that would be helpful
and practical in their everyday lives. This desire to be helpful
was no less true with the retrocognitive information. Even
as interesting as some of the historical information may be,
however, the real question is "Was the life reading material
helpful to those who received it?" Repeatedly, documentation within the Cayce files describes how the information
helped them, turned their lives around, or even saved them
from disaster. In one case a young man [2157] sought help
and direction from a life reading. His parents later reported:

Report from 1953: "He was floundering at 19—not knowing
what to make his life work. Background of seafaring men—
did not care to follow the sea…As a result of the reading he
took up aviation and was very successful from the start—flew
all through the war—was a flight engineer on a B-24. Went
into aviation after the war and has made splendid headway in
one of the larger companies in the Midwest." 2157-1 Reports

What information had been so helpful to the young
man? In addition to confirming his adversity to "water and

waterways, water activities," the reading discussed his "floundering" and suggested an outlet different from the rest of
his family's. The young man also asked for some "spiritual
advice," which was given:

In giving the interpretations of the records as we find
them here, these are chosen with the desire and purpose
that this may be a helpful experience for the entity.

For the entity, while in the material experiences
accomplished a very great deal in some phases of the activity, at times there has been a lacking in those things as
might stabilize same.

Thus in the present we will find periods when apparently there is failure to arrive at those points of contact
or conclusions as desired. Yet if these are carried in the
spiritual as well as the mental, the material import and
material application, there will come those experiences
wherein the entity will again be quoted as an authority respecting phases of that which as we find will prove
the greater channel of activity of the entity during this
experience—aviation ...

(Q) Any spiritual advice?
(A) As indicated through the experiences and sojourns, those
variations that have come in the astrological urges are from
the lack of the spiritual application of the truths known. Do
not make such a failure in this experience. 2157-1

Sometimes information from the past came unexpectedly. In 1932, at the end of an emergency reading for Mrs. [1315], who had suffered a painful and sleepless night, Cayce did not come out of the trance state despite the suggestion given three times for him to wake up. Instead, somehow he became a witness to the events of the Last Supper, which the reading described. A later reading suggested that the spiritual attunement of those present had made the experience possible:

The Lord's Supper—here with the Master—see what they had for supper—boiled fish, rice, with leeks, wine, and loaf. One of the pitchers in which it was served was broken—the handle was broken, as was the lip to same.

The whole robe of the Master was not white, but pearl gray—all combined into one—the gift of Nicodemus to the Lord.

The better looking of the twelve, of course, was Judas, while the younger was John—oval face, dark hair, smooth face—only one with the short hair. Peter, the rough and ready—always that of very short beard, rough, and not altogether clean; while Andrew's is just the opposite—very sparse, but inclined to be long more on the side and under the chin—long on the upper lip—his robe was always near gray or black, while his clouts or breeches were striped; while those of Philip and Bartholomew were red and brown.

The Master's hair is 'most red, inclined to be curly in

portions, yet not feminine or weak—*strong*, with heavy piercing eyes that are blue or steel-gray.

His weight would be at least a hundred and seventy pounds. Long tapering fingers, nails well kept. Long nail, though, on the left little finger.

Merry—even in the hour of trial. Joke—even in the moment of betrayal.

The sack is empty. Judas departs.

The last is given of the wine and loaf, with which He gives the emblems that should be so dear to every follower of Him. Lays aside His robe, which is all of one piece— girds the towel about His waist, which is dressed with linen that is blue and white. Rolls back the folds, kneels first before John, James, then to Peter—who refuses.

Then the dissertation as to "He that would be the greatest would be servant of all."

The basin is taken as without handle, and is made of wood. The water is from the gherkins [gourds], that are in the wide-mouth Shibboleths [streams? Judges 12:6], that stand in the house of John's father, Zebedee.

And now comes "It is finished."

They sing the ninety-first Psalm—"He that dwelleth in the secret place of the Most High shall abide under the shadow of the Almighty. I will say of the Lord, He is my refuge and my fortress: my God; in Him will I trust."

He is the musician as well, for He uses the harp.

They leave for the garden. 5749-1

Interestingly enough, thirty-two years later, in March 1964, *Woman's Life* magazine printed a "Letter to Tiberius" that was reported to have been written nearly two thousand years earlier from a Roman citizen, Publius Lentulus, to his emperor, Tiberius. The original letter had remained in the Roman archives but had not been translated until later. The account provided an amazingly similar description of Jesus to the one that had been given by the readings thirty years before. It reads:

There has appeared in Palestine a man who is still living and whose power is extraordinary. He has the title given him of Great Prophet, his disciples call him "Son of God." He raises the dead and heals all sorts of diseases.

He is a tall, well-proportioned man, and there is an air of severity in his countenance which at once attracts the love and reverence of those who see him. His hair is the colour of new wine from the roots to the ears, and thence to the shoulders it is curled and falls down to the lowest part of them. Upon the forehead, it parts in two after the manner of Nazarenes. His forehead is flat and fair, his face without blemish or defect, and adorned with a graceful expression. His nose and mouth are very well proportioned, his beard is thick and the colour of his hair. His eyes are grey and extremely lively. In his reproofs, he is terrible, but in his exhortations and instructions, amiable and courteous. There is something wonderfully charming in this face with a mixture of gravity. He is never seen to laugh, but has been observed to weep. He is very straight in stature, his hands large and spreading, his arms are very beautiful. He talks little, but with a great quality and is the handsomest man in the world. 5749-1 Reports

Not everyone who received a life reading was immediately convinced of the accuracy of Cayce's retrocognitive information. One example is the case of a fourteen-year-old boy who had been given the reading as a birthday present from his older sister. The reading stated that, in past incarnations, the boy had frequently been involved in the material and clothing business. It was in this very line of work, Cayce claimed, that the individual would have his greatest degree of financial success and positive business interactions with other people. However, nothing about the career even appealed to the youth. Even when he became a young man, he still showed no interest:

On 8/22/34: "At the age of twenty-one, Case [641]—was still working with the small-town newspaper, although he had risen to the position of assistant circulation manager. He was making only a moderate salary and was then the chief support of his mother and a younger sister; he reported that he had no opportunity to get into the line of work suggested by the reading and, besides, he could feel no special inclination or urge in that direction. It was hard for him to understand why the reading advised a life's work which had no appeal for him. However, he felt that he was at a standstill in his present position and saw no chance for advancement; consequently he was seeking a change of some kind." 641-1 Reports

Seven years earlier, Cayce's reading had included the following information about the man's past, suggesting that it laid the groundwork for his potential future:

One that, then, without respect of will, finds these conditions as urges in the present experience:

One that will find the greater success, the greater development in the present experience, coming through that of association with peoples—in the condition of the *business* man, especially that as pertains to materials, clothing, or of such natures. These will be the natural trend and bent of the entity in its relations with individuals and things, for with that of the ability to make friends, and of the turn that is seen in the *nobleness* of purpose, this will offer the channel through which the greater development in the moral, the physical, the financial, the spiritual way, may come in this present experience. Hence the training that the entity should have under such conditions and relations should begin as soon as this may. Either by that of the gradual development into the association of, or to get—as it were—the correct groundwork for such a development...

In those experiences in the earth's plane, and the urges as are seen from same:

In the one before this we find in that period when the peoples in the land now known as France were near to the rebellion, in the period of Louis the 13th. The entity then among those who were as the escorts and protectors of that monarch, and was *especially* the one that chose for that ruler the dress or the change of apparel—though *not* in the capacity of the valet. *Rather* as one who set the styles for the peoples. In the name then Neil [?] and the entity gained through this experience, giving of self in service in the way and manner as was in keeping with the period, and not acting in any manner other than that of the correct in mien and in position. The urge as is seen—particular with self as to dress, and the ability to well describe the dress of a whole room full of peoples, [if the body will] set self or *think*, as it were, concerning same...

In the one before this we find in that period known as the division in the kingdom in the land now known as Egyptian. The entity then among those peoples that were of the native folk, yet the one that brought much comfort to many peoples in providing for the application of the truth as was given by those in rule so that the native understood the intent and purpose. Acting then in the capacity of the teacher, the minister, or the go-between between the priests of the day and the common people. Hence among those who first in the land took on especial class of raiment or garments to designate self from other peoples, being appointed or given this permission through those in power, both religious and political. In the name Isois, and there is seen yet among the Egyptian ruins or relics reference made to the entity's application of self to the peoples...641-1

Later, in the spring of 1939, Mr. [641] was visiting some friends of his sister in another city. For three generations, the entire family had been involved in the clothing and uniform business. Aware of Edgar Cayce and the information provided in [641]'s reading, the family offered him a job as a traveling salesman. Desiring a change of some kind, he decided to accept. The results were extremely gratifying. Even in the first year, his success was phenomenal. There seemed to be something very special about [641]'s knack with other people. In fact, the family who hired him said his talent was not matched by any of their other employees. For more than thirty years, until his retirement, he worked for the company and proved to be a great success. In fact, toward the end of his career, he took on the responsibility of training salesmen for the national organization.

Cayce had done it again.

CHAPTER 6

DREAMS, VISIONS, AND OTHER EXPERIENCES

In addition to the readings that deal with the categories of telepathy, clairvoyance, precognition, and retrocognition, a number of Cayce's other psychic experiences seem to require a category of their own. For the sake of simplicity, these have been labeled "dreams, visions, and other experiences."

The Edgar Cayce material places a great deal of emphasis on the importance of dreams. Each of us is much more aware of ourselves, our surroundings, even our relationships at a subconscious level than we can possibly imagine, and these insights can be tapped in the dream state. The readings suggest that dreams are a purposeful experience and that "all visions and dreams are given for the benefit of the individual, would they but interpret them correctly..." (295-15).

Often, while in the trance state and giving a reading for someone else, Cayce would have a dream which he would describe upon awakening. Frequently, a reading would be procured at a later date on the dream itself. On occasion, the reading would state that much more than a simple dream had occurred, that the experience had been a "vision"—an actual experience with which a portion of Cayce's consciousness had been involved.

More than one hundred of Cayce's personal dreams are contained within his case files. As stated earlier, perhaps one of his most frequently discussed dreams was the one in which he saw himself being born again in the year A.D. 2158 in a coastal town in Nebraska! In the dream, even though the date was years in the future, records of Edgar Cayce's life and work continued to exist. The dream occurred after an arrest and a court date in Detroit for practicing medicine without a license. At the time of the dream, Cayce had been depressed and discouraged, wondering about the future of his Work. A reading was given on the dream, stating that the dream's most important purpose was to demonstrate the fact that his Work was important and meaningful and would survive:

This then is the interpretation. As has been given, "Fear not." Keep the faith; for those that be with thee are greater than those that would hinder. Though the very heavens fall, though the earth shall be changed, though the heavens shall pass, the promises in Him are sure and will stand—as in that day—as the proof of thy activity in the lives and hearts of those of thy fellow man. 294-189

Another of Edgar Cayce's more notable dreams occurred repeatedly over the years. It was a dream that portrayed his entering into the trance state, traveling through the various levels of consciousness, arriving at the place that contained the akashic records, and being handed the particular information that he was seeking. While giving a lecture in 1933, Edgar Cayce described the experience:

> I see myself as a tiny dot out of my physical body, which lies inert before me. I find myself oppressed by darkness and there is a feeling of terrific loneliness. Suddenly, I am conscious of a white beam of light. As this tiny dot, I move upward following the light, knowing that I must follow it or be lost.
>
> As I move along this path of light I gradually become conscious of various levels upon which there is movement. Upon the first levels there are vague, horrible shapes, grotesque forms such as one sees in nightmares. Passing on, there begin to appear on either side misshapen forms of human beings with some part of the body magnified. Again there is change and I become conscious of gray-hooded forms moving downward. Gradually, these become lighter in color. Then the direction changes and these forms move upward and the color of the robes grows rapidly lighter. Next, there begin to appear on either side vague outlines of houses, walls, trees, etc., but everything is motionless. As I pass on, there is more light and

movement in what appear to be normal cities and towns. With the growth of movement I become conscious of sounds, at first indistinct rumblings, then music, laughter, and singing of birds. There is more and more light, the colors become very beautiful, and there is the sound of wonderful music. The houses are left behind, ahead there is only a blending of sound and color. Quite suddenly I come upon a hall of records. It is a hall without walls, without ceiling, but I am conscious of seeing an old man who hands me a large book, a record of the individual for whom I seek information. 294-19 Reports

A very practical dream experience (294-189 Reports) came when Cayce suffered from a cough and cold. One night he had a dream that prescribed a cough medicine for him to take and gave the ingredients and appropriate measures for each: 4 tablespoons of boiling water, 1 tablespoon of honey, 1 tablespoon of compound simple syrup, 10 drops of glycerin, 2 drops of creosote, 1 teaspoon syrup of horehound, 15 drops of tolu in solution, 30 drops of compound tincture benzoin, and 2 ounces of whiskey. The formula was prepared, and his cough was relieved.

In a lengthy dream recorded on December 19, 1919, Cayce had an unusual experience. Later, he asked in a reading whether the experience had been a vision or a dream. The answer was that it contained elements of both:

SCENE 1:

Apparently, there was spread before me all the graveyards in the world. I saw nothing save the abode of what we call the dead, in all portions of the world.

SCENE 2:

Then, as the scene shifted, the graves seemed to be centered around India, and I was told by a voice somewhere, "Here you will know a man's religion by the manner in which his body has been disposed of."

SCENE 3:

The scene then changed to France, and I saw the soldiers' graves, and among them the grave of 3 boys who had been in my [Sunday school] class. Then I saw the boys, not dead but alive. Each of them told me how they met their death; one in machine gun fire, another in the bursting of a shell, the other in the heavy artillery fire. Two gave me messages to tell their loved ones at home. They appeared much in the same way and manner as they did the day each came to bid me good-bye.

SCENE 4:

As the scene changed again, I apparently reasoned with myself, "This is what men call spiritualism. Can it be true? Are all those we call dead yet alive in some other plane of experience or existence? Could I see my own baby boy?" [A son, Milton Porter Cayce, had died shortly after birth.]

As if a canopy was raised, tier on tier of babies appeared. In the 3rd or 4th row from the top, to the side, I recognized my own child. He knew me, even as I knew him. He smiled his recognition, but no word of any kind passed.

SCENE 5:

The scene changed, and there appeared a lady friend who was being buried in the local cemetery during that self-same hour, one whom I had known very well and from whom I had purchased many flowers for distribution by the children in my [Sunday school] classes. She talked with me about the changes that men call death, said that it was a real birth. Especially she spoke concerning the effect the gift of flowers had upon individuals, and how they should be given in life rather than at funerals or death. As to what they meant, and how they spoke to the invalid, the shut-ins, and meant so little to those that had passed from material to the spiritual plane. Then she said, "But to be material for the moment, some months ago someone left $2.50 with you for me. You are not aware of this having been done, and will find it in a drawer of your desk marked with the date it was paid, Aug. 8th, and there are 2 paper dollars with a 50 cent piece. See that my daughter receives this, for she will need it. Be patient with the children, they are gaining much."

SCENE 6:

Again the scene changed, and there appeared a man [4971] who had been a fellow officer for years in the church of which I was a member. He spoke of his son [228], who was a very close friend of mine, but was soon to return from the army, saying that he would no doubt return to his place in the local bank but advising that he rather accept the offer which would be made from a moving [movie] picture house. Then he spoke concerning the affairs of the church, and then I was physically conscious again. 294-15 Reports

Edgar Cayce's conscious report of the above experience follows:

IN RE[GARDS] TO SCENE 5:

I went to my office and looked in the drawer of the desk where I was told to look and, sure enough, there was the envelope that had been received on the 8th of August by one of the young ladies who had since left the [photography] studio (and this was in December).

IN RE[GARDS] TO SCENE 6:

The next day I had occasion to go to the bank and the young man, my friend, took my deposit. I asked when he returned, and he said last night. I asked if he expected to remain in the bank and he said he thought so. Then I told him I had something I would like to relate to him, and that he could act as he felt right. He came to the studio within the hour, and I related to him the whole experience. He told me that on his way home from Washington he had stopped in Atlanta, that he had been approached by a friend and asked to take the management of a moving picture theatre, but he had that morning mailed him a letter rejecting the offer, but that he would immediately wire him accepting it—which he did...

IN RE[GARDS] TO SCENES I THROUGH 4:
This one thing I do know. I have traveled in many portions of the country, north, south, east, and west. There are few, if any, cemeteries, that do not appear familiar, so much so yet that when I see even a corner of one I can with a few minutes' reflection tell many intimate things about that particular cemetery... 294-15 Reports

Confirming the fact that the dead are still very much alive—simply in another plane of consciousness—Edgar Cayce related an experience he once had with a woman *after* she had been dead for some fifteen years!

Awoke one evening [1935–1936?] with a rapping on the window, realized it was some one, arose, slipped on my dressing gown, went to the window and asked who is it and [in] a very distinct voice she answered, giving me her nickname, telling me she wished to talk with me, to come down and let her in, which I did. Talked with her just as would any friend, for an hour, a very natural voice. A very real personality. There are many questions I wonder that I did not ask...I might have thought this experience just a dream it was so real, except that the [secretary] here was still at work in the office here in the home, saw me go down, heard me open the door, and heard voices during the time she was here...1196-1

On another occasion, Edgar Cayce related an experience he witnessed while giving a sermon to his Sunday school class at the Presbyterian Church (294-155 Reports). While he was speaking, he saw a number of robed figures enter the church and stand, listening to his complete discourse. From their attire, he recognized them as members of the Jewish faith. No one else in the church saw them. A reading stated later that these people had simply been interested in his topic and they had come to hear the lecture—the vision was real.

Another vision occurred one day while Cayce was tending to his garden. An apparition appeared to him in the sky:

I was in the garden here at work when I heard a noise like the noise of a swarm of bees. When I looked to see where they were, I saw that the noise came from a chariot in the air with 4 white horses and a driver. I did not see the face of the driver. The experience lasted only a few minutes. I was trying to persuade myself that it was not true, that it was only imagination, when I heard a voice saying, "Look behind you." I looked and beheld a man in armor, with a shield, a helmet, knee guards, a cape but no weapon of any kind. His countenance was like the light; his armor was as silver or aluminum. He raised his hand in salute and said, "The chariot of the Lord and the horsemen thereof." Then he disappeared. I was really weak, not from fright but from awe and wonder. It was a most beautiful experience and I hope I may be worthy of many more. 294-185

A reading confirmed that the experience had been a conscious vision and that it had occurred to demonstrate the ever-existent presence of the Lord—even during those moments when Cayce felt "periods of oppression."

In 1926 Edgar Cayce had a personal experience—one of many—that confirmed for him the process of reincarnation. While giving a reading for an infant, Cayce stated that, in the life just previous to the present, the child [318] had been "Thomas Cayce"—Edgar Cayce's little brother who had died when Edgar was only fifteen. Later, when a man wrote Cayce asking for what evidence there was for reincarnation, Cayce related the story:

Letter of 1/5/43 from Edgar Cayce to Mr. [4959]:

"...years ago, many years I had a little brother. He lived only a few months—his was the first time death touched me—and as the child I did not understand—who does? Save, 'In the day ye eat there of ye shall surely die.' Time went on eventually some theory that reincarnation was presented in the information. I prayed earnestly about same, asked to be shown the truth, earnestly, sincerely, and I believe God hears prayer. Eventually, I had a very good friend—we will say a Mr. [779] and his family—a wife [780], and three lovely children—he was in my [Sunday school] class. He and each member of his family had more than once come to the information for help—and apparently had gotten same...a boy [318] was born. They asked for a reading...[The child was confirmed to be Thomas Cayce. Edgar Cayce did not see him again until he was two and a half years old.]

[At that time] He merely stood off and looked intently at me. Then, suddenly he rushed to me with his little face radiant and said, 'Brother.' What that did to me, [4959], can never tell any one! He at once began to beg me to take him home with me—that he belonged to me, that he didn't belong there. I had to leave while he was asleep—I could not interfere. I know he was there for a purpose, what Who knows did not see him again until he was past ten. Then was in the home again...When I went to leave, he was packed to leave with me without saying anything. Then I tried to talk with him, told him how necessary he was in that home and he must finish school there. He was resigned. Incredible story, [4959], but every word true, so help me God! Had you had that experience, what would you say? And that my friend, is only one of hundreds [I] have experienced in the last 15 years. No, no, no, not proof to anyone but mighty meaningful to me...2722-5 Reports

In addition to being able to give readings in the trance state, Edgar Cayce was extremely psychic in the waking state. One of his psychic talents was his ability to see *auras*—patterns of light that emanate from people (and even other living things) and contain information regarding their health, their frame of mind, even events in their lives. As a demonstration of this perceptive ability, on the night of August 26, 1941, at his Tuesday night Bible class, Edgar Cayce went around the room and described the auras of those in attendance (5746-1 Reports). Although more than twenty people were present, only a few of the comments given that night to specific individuals are recorded here in order to give an indication of what took place:

To [2533]: You have more violet in your aura than anyone in the room. Violet always indicates the seeker, the searcher for something. You have more of [violet] than gray, blue, opal, white or pink. A great deal of pink or coral in an individual's aura indicates material-mindedness...

To [845]: You have a light more than you have an aura. There is a light that stays about you now, which may become a part of your aura or it may be a thing that you are attaining to. But there's more of a white light that stays about you as an aura. Not many people have a white light, because when most people attain to a white light they are getting ready to do something in the way of individual accomplishment; that is, it represents that surety in which an individual has put a hope—and such an environ is created about the individual. It is not a ball of light, but more a shaft of light—that with your dark hair appears to be almost white.

To [404]: The last time I read your aura there were a lot of shadows about it. Now it is entirely different. I would see from your aura that you have some very unusual news coming to you. This is indicated by the way in which your aura circles about the head—a circle and one above it, and one above it; more like we usually picture a halo—a streak of gold, as that especially about a picture of the Master. There is gold and white, which would indicate good news.

To [1523]: You have a very unusual sort of aura at present. There is a great deal of gray and blue and gold. Yours is mighty high sometimes and down mighty low at other times. It is very much like a crown, but a crown with spikes—a circular crown with spikes. Violet, opal, gray, and tipped off with gold. So at times you make snap judgments, at other times you give due consideration, at other times you don't give a cuss! This is indicated by the difference in the shading of the spikes; there are two shades of red, two shades of gray, two shades of blue—in those variations…5746-1 Reports

Although the vast majority of Edgar Cayce's psychic ability was demonstrated in the trance state, throughout his life, he had conscious experiences that extended beyond the bounds of "normal" perception. In fact, these experiences had occurred all the way back to his childhood. It is not unusual for children to believe they have invisible friends, and Edgar

Cayce was no exception. As an adult, he occasionally spoke about the "invisible playmates" he had seen as a child. One woman, Mrs. [464], had heard about these experiences and the fact that Cayce had been called "a strange child" because of them. Her oldest daughter had brought home from the library a book about fairies by Sir Arthur Conan Doyle. When her daughter asked for more information, the woman wrote Cayce and asked if he would mind detailing some of his personal experiences. His letter of January 31, 1933, follows:

Yours of the 27th has been received. The questions you ask are very interesting and, to me, very much worth while. All through the years I think I have been (possibly from necessity) quite a matter of fact individual. No doubt all my childhood and boyhood associates were also quite matter of fact. Consequently, I have gotten far away from many of the experiences that were very near and dear to me as a little child. As I look back upon the various experiences I rather persuade myself they have been steps in my development. Perhaps if I had paid more attention to them the present would be quite different.

I don't know whether or not I can give you sufficient insight to be worth while, as to just what took place during those experiences of my early childhood when I visited unseen playmates; for I will have to admit that—except for a general outline of my life, in which this subject is touched on just a little—I have never attempted to put those experiences in writing. So, if my letter appears some-what disconnected or unreasonable, know that it is because of a physically developed body (and possibly a sane mind) attempting to keep within the bounds of reason. Except the fairy stories of Grimm and Hans [Christian] Andersen, I have never read of others' experiences. While I have had a little correspondence with Sir Arthur Conan Doyle, and have one or two of his books, I have not read the one you mention. I would love very much to read it, and will see if my son can obtain it from the Norfolk library.

These are at least some of my experiences. As to just what was the first experience, I don't know. The one that appears at present to be among the first, was when I was possibly eighteen or twenty months old. I had a playhouse in the back of an old garden, among the honeysuckle and other flowers. At that particular time much of this garden had grown up in tall reeds, as I remember. I had made a little shelter of the tops of the reeds, and had been assisted by an unseen playmate in weaving or fastening them together so they would form a shelter. On pretty days I played there. One afternoon my mother came down the garden walk calling me. My playmate (who appeared to me to be about the same size as myself) was with me. It had never occurred to me that he was not real, or that he wasn't one of the neighbors' children, until my mother spoke and asked me my playmate's name. I turned to ask him but he disappeared. For a time this disturbed my mother somewhat, and she questioned me at length. I remember crying because she had spied upon me several times, and each time the playmate would disappear.

About a year or eighteen months later, this was changed considerably—as to the number of playmates. We had moved to another country home. Here I had two favorite places where I played with these unseen people. One (very peculiarly) was in an old graveyard where the cedar trees had grown up. Under a cedar tree, whose limbs had grown very close to the ground, I made another little retreat, where—with these playmates—I gathered bits of colored glass, beautifully colored leaves and things of that nature from time to time. But, what disturbed me was that I didn't know where they came from nor why they left when some of my family approached. The other retreat was a favorite old strawstack that I used to slide down. This was on the opposite side of the road (main highway) from where we lived, and in front of the house. The most outstanding experience (and one that I am sure disturbed her much) was when my mother looked out a window and saw children sliding down this strawstack with me. Of course, I had a lovely little retreat dug out under the side of the straw ring, in which we often sat and discussed the mighty problems of a three or four year old child. As my mother looked out, she called to ask who were the children playing with me. I realized I didn't know their names. How were they dressed, you ask? There were boys and girls. It would be impossible (at this date) to describe their dress, figure or face, yet it didn't then—nor does it now—occur to me that they were any different from myself, except that they had the ability to appear or disappear as our moods changed. Just once I looked out the window from the house and saw the fairies there, beckoning me to come and play. That time also my mother saw them very plainly, but she didn't make any objection to my going out to play with them. This experience, as I remember now, lasted during a whole season—or summer.

A few years afterwards (when I had grown to be six or seven years old) our home was in a little wood. Here I learned to talk with the trees, or it appeared that they talked with me. I even yet hold that anyone may hear voices, apparently coming from a tree, if willing to choose a tree (a living tree, not a dead one) and sit against it for fifteen to twenty minutes each day (the same time each day) for twenty days. This was my experience. I chose a very lovely tree, and around it I played with my playmates that came (who then seemed very much smaller than I). We built a beautiful bower of hazelnut branches, redwood, dogwood and the like, with wild violets, Jack-in-the-Pulpit, and many of the wild mosses that seemed to be especially drawn to this particular little place where I met my friends to talk with—the little elves of the trees. How often this came, I don't know. We lived there for several years. It was there that I read the Bible through the first time, that I learned to pray, that I had many visions or experiences; not only of visioning the elves but what seemed to me to be the hosts that must have appeared to the people of old, as recorded in Genesis particularly. In this little bower there was never any intrusion from those outside. It was here that I read the first letter from a girlfriend. It was here that I went to pray when my grandmother died, whom I loved so dearly and who had meant so much to me. To describe these elves of the trees, the fairies of the woods, or—to me—the angels or hosts, with all their beautiful and glorious surroundings, would be almost a sacrilege. They have meant, and do yet, so very much to me that they are as rather the sacred experiences that we do not speak of—any more than we would of our first kiss, and the like. Why do I draw such comparisons? There are, no doubt, physical manifestations that are a counterpart or an expression of all the unseen forces about us, yet we have closed our eyes and our ears to the songs of the spheres, so that we are unable again to hear the voices or to see the forms take shape and minister—yea strengthen us—day by day!

Possibly there are many questions you would ask, as to what games we played. Those I played with at the haystack were different from those in the graveyard, or in the garden. Those I played with in the wood were different. They seemed to fit more often to what would interest or develop me. To say they planted the flowers or selected the bower, or the little cove in which my retreat was built, I don't think would be stretching it at all, or that they tended these or showed me—or talked to me of—their beauty. It was here that I first learned to read. Possibly the hosts on high gave me my first interpretation of that we call the Good Book. I do not think I am stretching my imagination when I say such a thing. We played the games of children, we played being sweethearts, we played being man and wife, we played being sisters and brothers, we played being visitors and preachers. We played being policemen and the culprits. We played being all the things that we knew about us. No, I never have any of these visions now, or—if any—very rarely...

But, as all such experiences, it was gradually explained away by our beautiful material-mindedness—saying it was nothing but imagination and the like.

What it all means, I don't know that I can comprehend or understand. As I have said to you before, all manifestations must be of that divine influence or force we call God. All forms of life, seen and unseen, are essences and manifestations of that One. *He* would gather us together, as the Master said "even as a hen gathereth her chickens under her wing, but ye will not!" We are so cocksure of ourselves, we want to stand alone.

Now, I hope all this reminiscing will at least be worth while. It is only my experience. I'm not asking anyone to believe it. We can't experience for another. We may only see the effects of what another has visioned or experienced, in the manner of life lived by another—and then judge by that which the individual has set as the standard...

We are having a lovely day here; it certainly makes me feel like getting out and digging in the earth—though it's a little bit damp yet, from our rain, wind and storm, for anything of the kind.

Let us hear from you whenever you have the opportunity. Know that we are always anxious and glad to hear from you. We hope we may in some manner say something, do something, be something, that will give a little hope and help to you in some way or manner.

> *All send our kindest regards.*
> *Sincerely, Edgar Cayce*
> *464-12 Reports*

On March 21, 1926, Edgar Cayce had a dream in which he saw himself scalding to death in a bathtub. A reading was given in which Cayce suggested that the interpretation had to do with "First and foremost—the *physical* defects in the body that need physical attention..." (294-70) Later, the reading told Cayce that, even after his death, his Work would continue: "...the operation of the work, as is seen and carried on in this state, *will be* going just the same..." In addition to pointing out physical problems that he was then experiencing, could the dream of death in the bathtub have foretold his method of passing away twenty years later? When Edgar Cayce died, on January 3, 1945, the cause diagnosed by the physician was "pulmonary edema"—water on the lungs.

CONCLUSION

Throughout his life, Edgar Cayce demonstrated the uncanny ability to put his mind into a state of consciousness that extended far beyond ordinary sense perception. Over the years, his readings discussed an amazing ten thousand different subjects. Because of the vast scope of this material, it isn't possible to present a complete listing of Cayce's psychic experiences in one volume. However, all of the information remains open to the public for professional research or for more casual investigation.

Even today, many misperceptions exist regarding the nature of psychic information. Somehow, the word *psychic* has been misunderstood to mean something out of the ordinary, something special, unusual, weird, or even infallible. None of these definitions corresponds with the approach of the Edgar Cayce readings. To Cayce, psychic ability was a natural talent of the soul. From his perspective, we are not simply physical bodies; instead, we are spiritual beings with unbounded consciousness potential who happen to be having a physical experience. Psychic information is simply information that comes to us through our extended sense perception. In addition, it is not necessarily 100 percent accurate. We all have filters, biases, and misperceptions to which the information is subject. In fact, a book written by Cayce's own sons, *The Outer Limits of Edgar Cayce's Power*, attempted to explore this very phenomenon in the Cayce readings.

For some reason, no one expects a talented business executive to *always* be correct when making decisions; no one expects a good parent to *always* exercise perfect discipline and judgment; no one believes that a talented minister can *always* deliver an inspiring sermon every time—yet we expect something very different from people who call themselves psychic. Because of the misunderstanding of what psychic ability is (as well as what it is not), many people either disregard the information altogether or they elevate it to an unreasonable level. From Cayce's perspective, we may wish to work with psychic information to the same degree that we would listen to the advice of a trusted friend. It can be used as an additional tool for gathering insights and for making decisions. It should not necessarily be given any more credence than any other form of guidance or counsel; however, it should not be given any less credence either.

Edgar Cayce never tried to distinguish himself as the world's greatest psychic. In fact, his emphasis was not on the phenomena of the readings themselves but rather on his desire to be helpful to people. The readings never offered a set of beliefs or principles that needed to be embraced or were infallible; rather, they presented an approach in which each individual was encouraged to test the information in his or her own life. With that in mind, the Association for Research and Enlightenment, Inc., was founded in 1931 as an association interested in facilitating personal inquiry and investigation into the Cayce material. That remains its purpose to this day.

When Cayce was still alive, inquirers into his Work received a booklet entitled *Edgar Cayce: His Life and Work.* Contained within it was a letter from Cayce that appropriately summed up his personal outlook regarding his Work:

> My friends, the life of a person endowed with such powers is not easy. For more than forty years now I have been giving readings for those who came seeking help. Thirty-five years ago the jeers, scorn and laughter were even louder than today. I have faced the laughter of ignorant crowds, the withering scorn of tabloid headlines, and the cold smirk of self-satisfied individuals. But I have also known the wordless happiness of little children who have been helped, the gratitude of fathers and mothers and friends. There are few mails that do not bring me expressions of appreciation for new life, new hope, new ability, stimulated through the readings which have been applied, in

some individual's life. Trouble and worry and criticism mean very little at such times.

I believe that the attitude of the scientific world is gradually changing towards these subjects. Men in their respective fields are devoting time and effort to studying the laws that govern all kinds of psychic phenomena. Universities in this and other countries are carrying on advanced experiments. Psychical research must have open-minded, intelligent cooperation from scientists in many fields in order to be ultimately of lasting value in human experience. Our Association hopes to have some part in bringing about such cooperation.

There must be many questions in your mind, questions that can only be answered by a more thorough study of the readings themselves. Indeed, the final answers must come from your own experiences...

Under the Association for Research and Enlightenment, Inc., we are attempting to make a careful study of the phenomena of the readings and at the same time ever pass on to others that which is proven to be helpful in each member's experiences. I give myself to these studies and experiments knowing that many have been helped, and hoping that I may be a "channel of blessing" to each individual who comes with some physical, mental, or spiritual burden. This is my life.

Edgar Cayce
ca. 1942

CHRONOLOGY OF
EDGAR CAYCE'S LIFE

1877   Edgar Cayce is born on March 18 near Beverly, Kentucky, a small town eight miles south of Hopkinsville.

1880   Gertrude Evans is born on February 22 in Hopkinsville.

1881   On June 18 Edgar witnesses the horse accident that causes the death of his grandfather Thomas Jefferson Cayce. Afterward, the young boy claims he can see and speak with his deceased grandfather.

1884   Edgar Cayce starts school in Beverly.

1890   Visionary experience in which a lady appears to him. Afterward, he discovers that he is able to memorize his schoolbooks by sleeping on them.

1892   Edgar quits high school and works on the farm of his paternal grandmother. She dies in August.

1894   In January the family moves to Hopkinsville; Edgar is hired at Hopper Brothers bookstore.

1897   On March 14 he becomes engaged to Gertrude Evans.

1898   In June he loses his job and works in a dry goods store. In July he is employed by a large bookstore in Louisville, J. P. Morton & Co.

1899   Home for Christmas, Edgar decides to stay in Hopkinsville. He forms a partnership with his father, Leslie Cayce, to sell insurance.

1900   Edgar travels from town to town selling insurance, as well as books and stationery for J. P. Morton & Co. In March, a partial paralysis of the vocal cords makes him unable to speak beyond a whisper. In the fall, the Hopkinsville photographer offers him a job as apprentice in his studio.

1901   Hart, a traveling hypnotist and showman, is able to make Edgar speak normally under hypnosis. On March 31, Edgar gives his first psychic reading: with the help of Al Layne, he diagnoses his own difficulty and regains his voice. He starts giving readings for Layne's patients.

1902   In May he accepts a job in a bookstore in Bowling Green, sixty miles away. In August, Layne calls him back to Hopkinsville regarding a little girl called Aimee Dietrich. Her case will play a key role in the history of the Cayce readings. Layne visits him every Sunday to continue the readings for his patients.

1903   On June 17 he marries Gertrude Evans in Hopkinsville. They go to live in Bowling Green. Layne leaves Hopkinsville in order to become a professional osteopath.

1904   In September, Edgar opens a photographic studio with Frank Potter.

1905   On January 30 Gladys Davis is born in Centerville, Alabama. Local medical doctors study Edgar's psychic ability.

1906   In December a fire destroys artwork Edgar has on consignment.

1907   On March 16 Hugh Lynn, Edgar and Gertrude's oldest son, is born. In September, another fire wrecks the studio. His partner withdraws, but Edgar reopens it alone.

1908   Gertrude and Hugh Lynn return to Hopkinsville, while Edgar stays in Bowling Green to pay off the debts generated by the fires.

1909   In August, Edgar pays the last bill related to the debt and leaves Bowling Green. He spends some time in Hopkinsville with Gertrude and Hugh Lynn, then finds a job in Alabama as a photographer. At Christmas, he meets Dr. Wesley Ketchum during a short visit in Hopkinsville.

1910   On October 9 the *New York Times* publishes a long article on Edgar Cayce's psychic powers. Edgar comes back to Hopkinsville and opens a photographic studio. With Dr. Wesley Ketchum, Albert Noe, and Leslie Cayce, he forms the Psychic Reading Corporation. For the first time, he gives daily readings on medical cases.

1911   In February, Hearst's *Chicago Examiner* publicizes Edgar Cayce. In March, Edgar, Leslie Cayce, and Albert Noe go to Chicago for a few days, and Edgar gives readings for the paper. On March 28, Milton Porter, Edgar and Gertrude's second son, is born. The baby dies on May 17. Edgar works on the Dalton case, providing suggested treatment for a fractured kneecap. Gertrude develops severe tuberculosis. The readings save her life and enable her to recover fully.

1912   In January, Dr. Hugo Münsterberg, of Harvard, arrives in Hopkinsville to investigate Cayce's psychic talent. Edgar breaks his contract with Ketchum and Noe. Once again, he moves to Alabama to work as a photographer.

1913   He acquires his own studio in Selma, Alabama. In the fall, Gertrude and Hugh Lynn move to Selma.

1914   In January, Hugh Lynn severely burns his eyes while playing with flash powder in the studio. He regains his sight thanks to the readings.

1918   On February 9, Edgar Evans, Edgar and Gertrude's youngest son, is born.

1919   In order to raise money for building a hospital, Edgar forms a partnership with others seeking oil in Texas. He spends four years there, unsuccessfully.

1923   Edgar returns to Selma. On September 10 he hires a permanent secretary, Gladys Davis, then eighteen years old. From that time on, she will be part of the family. Arthur Lammers, from Dayton, requests a reading on astrology. It mentions the concept of reincarnation and opens up a whole new area of research. Invited by Lammers, in November, Edgar and his family move to Dayton, where he gives readings on philosophical, metaphysical, and astrological topics.

1925   Morton Blumenthal, a New York stockbroker, agrees to finance the hospital in Virginia Beach, Virginia, the location recommended by the readings. In September the Cayce family and Gladys Davis move to Virginia Beach.

1926   On October 26 Edgar's mother, Carrie Cayce, passes away.

1927   On May 6 the Association of National Investigators, Inc., is founded.

1928   On November 11 the Cayce Hospital is inaugurated.

1929   In October the stock market crash marks the onset of the Depression.

1930   On September 22 Atlantic University opens its doors.

1931   On February 26 the organization is dissolved. On February 28 the hospital closes. On July 7 the A.R.E., Association for Research and Enlightenment, Inc., was incorporated. By the end of the year, the university stops its activities. Readings on spiritual growth begin for the first study group.

1937   On April 11 Edgar's father, Leslie Cayce, passes away.

1942   In March, Edgar Cayce's biography *There Is a River*, by Thomas Sugrue, is published.

1944   On September 17 Cayce gives his last psychic reading, for himself.

1945   On January 3 Edgar Cayce dies at the age of sixty-seven. On April 1 Gertrude Evans Cayce dies at the age of sixty-five.

Kevin J. Todeschi is the CEO and executive director of the Association for Research and Enlightenment (A.R.E.), the educational organization founded by Edgar Cayce and one of the most popular growth centers in America, attracting thousands of visitors to its Virginia Beach campus each year. He additionally oversees activities of the A.R.E. worldwide. As both student and teacher of the Edgar Cayce material for more than thirty years, Todeschi has lectured on the Cayce teachings and related metaphysical topics on five continents. He is the author of more than twenty books, including *Edgar Cayce on the Akashic Records* and *Edgar Cayce on Soul Mates*. Todeschi has a master's degree in transpersonal psychology. He lives with his family in Virginia Beach, Virginia.

The Association for Research and Enlightenment, Inc. (A.R.E.®) is a not-for-profit organization founded in 1931 by Edgar Cayce to research and explore transpersonal subjects such as holistic health, philosophy, dreams and dream interpretation, intuition, and contemporary spirituality.

Although centered in the United States in Virginia Beach, Virginia, the A.R.E. community is a global network of individuals who offer conferences, educational activities, and fellowship around the world. More than 300 books have been written about Cayce's life and work, resulting in "Edgar Cayce Centers" in 37 countries and representatives in 70 countries.

In addition to study groups and local regional activities, A.R.E. offers membership benefits and services, a bimonthly magazine, a newsletter, publications, conferences, international tours, an impressive volunteer network, a massage school curriculum, a retreat-type camp for children and adults, impressive online resources, and A.R.E. contacts around the world. A.R.E. also maintains an affiliation with Atlantic University, which offers a master's degree program in Transpersonal Studies, as well as the Cayce/Reilly School of Massotherapy, which offers programs in massage therapy and health.

For additional information about programs and activities anywhere in the world, please contact the international headquarters in the United States: A.R.E., 215 67th Street, Virginia Beach, VA 23451-2061; call: (800) 333-4499; or check out the Web site at: www .EdgarCayce.org. You can also explore additional books about the life and work of Edgar Cayce at www.arebookstore.com.

EDGAR CAYCE'S ESP
Who He Was, What He Said, and How It Came True
Kevin J. Todeschi

One of the most remarkable stories of the twentieth century about one of the most incredible men who ever lived: Edgar Cayce, a Kentucky farm boy whose psychic powers healed thousands, touched countless lives, and inspired the dawn of the New Age. ISBN 978-1-58542-665-2

BUDDHA
His Life and His Teaching
Walter Henry Nelson

The thrilling story of one of the most inspiring figures in human history—a young prince who sacrificed wealth and power for self-knowledge and enlightenment: Gautama Buddha.
ISBN 978-1-58542-664-5